Dan Smith
12/24/03

Any

Native Dancer

by Eva Jolene Boyd

Lexington, Kentucky

THOROUGHBRED
Legends®
No. 7

ECLIPSE
PRESS

Library of Congress Card Number: 00-104790

ISBN 1-58150-048-3

Printed in The United States
First Edition: December 2000

a division of
The Blood-Horse, Inc.
PUBLISHERS SINCE 1916

To learn more about Native Dancer
and other classic Thoroughbreds, see:

www.thoroughbredlegends.com

NATIVE DANCER

CONTENTS

INTRODUCTION

The Gray Ghost

I n the book *Legends*, the renowned equine artist Richard Stone Reeves wrote: "Rarely do all elements come together to create such a star as Native Dancer." He mentioned two of those elements: television and Native Dancer's color complemented by the abundant dapples that Reeves said make for a "bright painting." He could have included pride, a champion's arrogance, and the "look" in the eyes. Native Dancer had it all. As Turf writer Joe Hirsch once said, "he was almost perfect."

Many associate Native Dancer with television. Indeed, he came along when that box with the small roundish screen invaded our homes and sat in our living rooms demanding our undivided attention. The 1951 Pimlico Special, won by Bryan G., was the first nationally televised horse race. And in 1952, the nation watched Hill Gail win the Kentucky Derby.

Early television viewers had a hard time identifying Thoroughbreds, most of which were browns, bays, or chestnuts, on their black and white screens. Then one April day in 1953, a national television audience tuned into the Gotham Stakes. Nine horses made up the field; eight of them looked alike. The ninth stood out like the proverbial ailing digit. He was a dappled gray with a large dark smudge in the middle of a face that was mostly white. He was easy to pick out, especially when he made his move. Racing columnist Red Smith wrote, "Native Dancer became the first national TV idol of his species, a frequent visitor in a million homes."

The more Native Dancer won, the more self-assured he became, an arrogance that allowed him to take his star status to another level. He added drama to his performances. Although he won all but three of his victories by open daylight, he often left his fans drained by making things look harder than they were.

"Time after time," wrote Charles Hatton for *The Morning Telegraph* and *Daily Racing Form*, "a vast nation-wide TV audience saw him in imminence of defeat, then snatch the brand from the burning in one astonishing rush."

Native Dancer was a "people's horse." Fan clubs sprang up all over the country, their members transcending generations and gender. He brought thousands of new fans to the sport, including this writer.

If only one word could describe him, it would be power. "He was without a doubt the strongest Thoroughbred I've ever seen in my life," said Ralph Kercheval, who managed Sagamore Farm. "...very strong in the shoulders and hindquarters. He was a power runner — not so much a graceful runner,"

George F. T. Ryall, Turf writer for *The New Yorker*, was impressed with him at first glance, saying he looked "every inch a champion. He has a fine head, is tall rather than long, deep through the heart, heavily muscled, and of magnificent carriage...His stride is immense."

He wasn't in full stride very often, but on those rare occasions, such as when he had to stretch out to catch Straight Face in the Metropolitan, railbirds swore they could see the bottoms of his feet. Early in 1953, a *LIFE* magazine photographer, using a large calibrated ruler marked in one-foot increments and set against the inside rail, measured Native Dancer's stride and found it to be a whopping twenty-nine feet, two feet longer than Man o' War's and five to seven feet longer than the average Thoroughbred's. Hatton attributed his stride to the colt's exceptional hind legs, which he described as "remarkably straight over the hock, with great length to the hip and short cannons."

Against a giant "V" adorned with his owner's colors, cerise and white diamonds, Native Dancer became the first of his kind to grace the cover of *TIME* magazine. The "V" likely stood for Vanderbilt, but could just as easily have stood for Victory. As Vanderbilt used to enjoy telling reporters, "You could fill a barn with horses that beat these other great runners; only one horse ever beat Native Dancer."

Hatton wrote that he was a Thoroughbred of "commanding presence." Such a presence can fill an artist's canvas and pull on the deepest emotions. One day at Belmont, hundreds of cheering fans lined the saddling paddock to see him. The Dancer reared, as if on cue. "That's the Gray Ghost!" they yelled, some seen to be in tears. "That's the champ!"

Color, ability, presence; all elements coming together to produce one of a kind.

CHAPTER 1

Better Late Than Never

For a good six months out of the year, Dan Scott didn't get much sleep.

As the owner of a Thoroughbred nursery and breeding farm, he had trained himself to sleep so lightly between January and June that a lamb's bleating would have awakened him. Calls from the foaling barn could come any time of the night, as one did shortly before two in the morning of March 27, 1950.

"Geisha is down," said the foaling barn's night watchman. There was no urgency in his voice, but the fact it was Geisha spurred Scott into quickly rising and hurriedly walking the short distance to the barn.

Scott made it a point to be on hand whenever any of the mares foaled, and he had particular interest in this one. Not that Alfred Vanderbilt's seven-year-old mare had displayed any difficulty, but she was twenty-eight days overdue, increasing the risk. Scott's own experience with late foals was good, however. He found that the youngsters tended to better resist infection.

At ten minutes after two, the roan mare delivered her baby uneventfully and proceeded to lick the youngster dry. Minutes later, the foal made the first awkward efforts to stand and then wobbled to his mother to nurse. He was nearly black, but as the baby coat dried and fluffed out, the tell-tale gray hairs around the muzzle and the tip of the tail indicated he would be a gray or a roan. Into the record book went the vital statistics:

Colt, gray or roan, 2:10 a.m., March 27, 1950. Polynesian—Geisha, by Discovery.

At Ira Drymon's Gallaher Farm just across the road, Polynesian dozed in his stall, unaware that his greatest offspring had just been born.

Geisha had arrived at Daniel Scott II's farm near Lexington, Kentucky, on December 16, 1949, to await the birth of her foal, after which she would be bred to Amphitheatre. Vanderbilt's mares customarily came here to foal because, as Sagamore Farm manager Ralph G. Kercheval explained of his lifelong friend's farm, "it was a nice place to be." And mares booked to Kentucky stallions would be available for breeding after foaling.

For the next three months, the big, leggy colt captured Scott's attention as he romped in the paddocks. But Scott admitted that he didn't predict anything out of the ordinary. "It would be nice to say I recognized his potentiality while he was a youngster," he recalled years later, "but that is not true."

However, he added, he did make it a point to watch late foals because of their extra vigor. Of the twenty-eight stakes winners foaled on the farm in the last twelve years, almost all had been overdue, Scott said.

Native Dancer experienced none of the usual ills and frailties of the average foal. Bigger than the other foals, he quickly established a pecking order, leaving little doubt as to who the "kingpin" was in his paddock. "He was a rough and ready guy," Scott remembered. "Whenever there was a ruckus among the foals, you could be sure he was right in the middle of it. He reveled in bullying the other youngsters, luring them away from their mothers. Yet he always managed to escape being hurt in any way."

Hot blood ran deep on Geisha's male side, with that terror of terrors Hastings only five generations back;

but Scott nixed any ideas the colt had a bad streak. "He was just a great big growing boy," he said.

On June 28, three months and one day after his arrival in the world, the colt was loaded onto a van with his mother, now in foal. They departed Kentucky for Sagamore Farm in Maryland.

Thirty-five years earlier, on the slanting decks of the mortally wounded liner *Lusitania*, Alfred Gwynne Vanderbilt Sr. must have pondered the fates that led him to this point. Just three years earlier, in 1912, he had canceled his passage on the *Titanic* because of a premonition the night before she sailed. What fortunes had saved him then only to bring him here?

Said in some quarters to be worth nearly $100 million, the son of Cornelius Vanderbilt and grandson of the 'Commodore' was an avid sportsman with an appetite for driving his $30,000 sports car at hair-raising speed over Florida beaches. But his first love was horses, and he divided his time between his U.S. and London stables, where he owned racing coach horses. He also was director of the International Horse Show Association, which had canceled its big fall show in England the year before because war had broken out with Germany. But the "war to end all wars" appeared to be going well now for the Allies, and the directors had decided to meet in London to plan the show's revival that fall. It was this meeting that had brought Vanderbilt to this fateful point.

In the fleeting minutes remaining in his young life, his thoughts likely were of the family he had left at the Vanderbilt Hotel in New York: his second wife, Margaret Emerson, and two sons, George and toddler Alfred. An older son, Billy, lived with his mother, Vanderbilt's first spouse.

Perhaps he recalled the warning in bold type that had appeared in New York newspapers on May 1 next to Cunard Line's announcement of *Lusitania*'s 10 a.m. sailing time. The warning from the Imperial German Embassy made it clear all ships flying England's flag were subject to attack by U-boats without warning.

"Why should we be afraid of German submarines?" Vanderbilt had responded with some impatience to reporters asking about the danger. "We can outdistance any submarine afloat." But it was the strange and cryptic telegram he and several other Americans received that morning — and dismissed as a hoax — that must have haunted him the most: "Have it on definite authority the *Lusitania* is to be torpedoed. You had better cancel passage immediately." [1]

Shortly after two on the afternoon of May 7, 1915, as the ship steamed up the English Channel on her way to Liverpool and passed just twelve miles off the Old Head of Kinsale on Ireland's southern coast, a torpedo hit her on the starboard side. Alone it was not a mortal blow, but the subsequent coal-dust explosion in an adjacent empty bunker ripped her open. The *Lusitania* quickly heeled over, still under steam. Having received warnings of submarine activity in the channel, Captain William Turner had ordered all the lifeboats swung out. There were more than enough for the people on board, but with her steep starboard list, the port side boats were useless. Women and children were pushed and thrown into the others. The liner went down in eighteen minutes taking with her nearly 1,200 souls, including some 124 Americans.

From several survivors' accounts, Vanderbilt was a hero. He had given his life jacket to someone else and then helped others with theirs. He could have made a go of it, but the thirty-eight-year-old sportsman, horse-man, race car driver could not swim a stroke.

Alfred Gwynne Vanderbilt Jr. was just two-and-a-half years old when his father died, but from his mother learned Vanderbilt Sr. had been a good and doting dad. And if passions are inherited along with eye color and height, then Alfred acquired more than the reported $8.5 million his father had left him (in four payments beginning when he was twenty-one and the last on his thirty-fifth birthday). He also inherited his love for horses. Though he often said it was the racing of horses he loved more.

Born in London on September 22, 1912, Alfred Jr. was ten years old when he went to his first horse race, the 1923 Preakness Stakes. With him was his maternal grandfather, Isaac Emerson, the Baltimore chemist who invented and then built Bromo-Seltzer into a fortune. He taught Alfred the basics of handicapping, and the lad placed his first dollar on a horse named Tall Timber, part of an entry with W. J. Salmon's Vigil. Tall Timber finished fifth but Vigil won, and Alfred collected half of the $11 paid on $2. Decades later, he recalled that day as the one that most endeared him to the sport.

"The first day I ever went to the races — the Preakness of 1923 — when I bet on a horse called Tall Timber, and a horse called Vigil won it, and it was an entry — which was news to me and my knee pants." Years later, Alfred would be president of Pimlico and more empathetic with the $2 bettor than the high roller.

When he was fourteen, he attended St. Paul's Academy in New Hampshire. While many of his classmates delighted in secretly perusing any reading materials on sex, Alfred's tastes ran to the *Daily Racing Form*, which arrived daily wrapped in discreet brown paper. At prep school in 1929, he took bets for that year's Kentucky Derby and scored big when no one picked the winner, Clyde Van Dusen. But curiously, the close call he had with his first dollar in the 1923 Preakness mellowed any desire he himself had for betting.

Then one day in 1932 at a paddock sale at Saratoga, Alfred, just nineteen at the time, impulsively bid on a two-year-old filly and got her for $250. She was a little thing, he recalled, and he named her Sue Jones. Later, *The Blood-Horse* printed this brief report: "The colors (cerise and white diamonds) of Alfred Vanderbilt, son of Mrs. Charles Amory, were shown in racing for the first time on June 16, when Sue Jones ran in the first race at Aqueduct." She ran third in that outing, but won a later race. Vanderbilt was hooked and dropped out of Yale University after only a year and a half.

His mother likely didn't protest. Margaret Emerson Vanderbilt had remarried twice since Alfred Sr.'s death, the second time becoming Mrs. Charles Minot Amory. Her father had invested some of the Bromo-Seltzer fortune into a grand horse facility near Baltimore and left it to Margaret. Under the name Sagamore Stable and the colors of cerise and white blocks, cerise sleeves, and white cap, Mrs. Amory sent two horses to the Kentucky Derby — Rock Man, who ran third to Bubbling Over in 1926, and Don Q, who didn't do nearly as well in Reigh Count's Derby two years later.

Since young Alfred was the only one of the boys interested in racing, Margaret presented him with Sagamore Farm on his twenty-first birthday in 1933. The affection she had for her second-born son is evident in a letter she wrote him on September 22.

"Alfred. 21 — and 'my man'! There is so much my dear I should be able to say to you. I have thought of so much I would say to you! & now the big day is here I can think of no words to express what I wanted to say!!…All I had to give, I gave to your father & he to me. You were very precious to him & had he lived possibly you would have had more advantages…Some unhappiness & worry will come into your life — it comes to us all — but meet it & learn to accept the bad with the good…remember always I am here to help you in any way I can. I wish you all the happiness in the whole world…I am proud of you…

"Always your devoted Mother."

Accompanying the letter was her gift to him:

"To Alfred G. Vanderbilt — I give, on Sept. 22, 1933, the Sagamore Racing Stable, with all contents — with all good wishes & with all his mother's love — Margaret E. Amory." [2]

The "contents" set up Alfred with sixteen broodmares, seven yearlings, two stallions, and a twenty-one-horse racing stable, plus the services of trainer J. H. (Bud) Stotler.

Despite the twenty-one runners already in hand, Vanderbilt promptly began looking for a promising two-year-old that he could point to next year's classics. On Stotler's advice, Vanderbilt found him — a big, powerful, flashy chestnut son of Display. His name was Discovery, and he would change Vanderbilt's life.

NATIVE DANCER

CHAPTER 2

Change And Discovery

O ne of the moments in his life that defined Alfred
Vanderbilt's love of racing came one fall day,
"…when I breezed the yearlings for the first time and
realized that the sons and daughters of Discovery really could run…" [1]

So could Discovery, who in most books ranks as one
of the top-four weight-carrying campaigners of the
20th Century, putting him in the company of
Exterminator, Kelso, and Forego.

He likely inherited some of that ability from fourth-
generation Hamburg, the sire of Discovery's third dam,
Adriana. Hamburg's juvenile campaign in 1897 reads
like that of a seasoned handicap runner. In sixteen
starts between June 7 and September 16, Hamburg
won twelve, in nine of which he carried 127 to 135
pounds, and as a three-year-old, he raced at distances

varying from seven furlongs to two and a quarter miles.

Discovery's sire line was loaded with talent and three generations of trouble; back to Hastings, who in the words of one contemporary, "...was born mad and never got real happy." Still, he was a decent racehorse and an excellent stallion. Fair Play was his best get, both as a runner and a stallion. He is so well-known as the sire of Man o' War that his accomplishments as a racehorse go unnoticed. Like Hastings, Fair Play's personality worsened at four; he refused to extend himself in six starts and was retired to owner August Belmont's Nursery Stud. When Belmont died in 1924, Fair Play moved to Joseph E. Widener's Elmendorf Farm, where he stood until his own death in 1929. Fair Play became the first stallion to get six $100,000 winners: Man o' War, Mad Hatter, Chance Shot, Mad Play, Chance Play, and Display, who could run all day.

But Display was a troublesome sort, low on patience with a short fuse. Bred by Walter J. Salmon of Mereworth Stud and foaled in 1923, Display loved to race, but usually spent most of his energy dragging assistant starters all over the track. Yet in 103 starts, he won twenty-three races and placed or showed in fifty-two others to retire with $256,526, second only to Zev's $313,639 on the American earnings list. Display was a better than fair sire, but none of his offspring could touch the chestnut colt from his first crop.

Discovery was striking in appearance: a powerfully built, brilliant chestnut with a wide blaze running from ears to muzzle. Discovery bore no resemblance to his tempestuous ancestor.

Foaled on March 3, 1931, Discovery, like his sire, was bred at Salmon's Mereworth Farm. He raced in the colors of Adolphe Pons, owner of Country Life Farm near Bel Air, Maryland, in his first thirteen starts at two, winning twice. Yet, as early as mid-season, trainer Bud Stotler liked him. When Vanderbilt began looking for a promising two-year-old to be his classic horse in 1934, Stotler recommended Discovery, who was already nominated for the Kentucky Derby. On October 29, 1933, the day after Discovery ran second to the grand filly Mata Hari by a neck in the Kentucky Jockey Club Stakes, he changed hands for $25,000. Carrying Vanderbilt's cerise and white diamonds for the first time, he ran second in the Walden Handicap on November 4, his final start for the year.

Discovery's only start prior to the Kentucky Derby was a third to Cavalcade in the Chesapeake Stakes. He went into the gate on May 5, 1934, as the sixth choice among thirteen starters for the Run for the Roses. With his twenty-one-year-old owner watching in disbelief, the colt led the heavily favored Cavalcade to the top of the stretch before giving way to the Brookmeade Stable runner. Although Discovery finished second, Vanderbilt remembered it as the biggest thrill in his young career.

"Everybody was trying to stand on the same chair I was," he recalled in 1940, "and everybody was yelling and Discovery was three on top as they turned into stretch. I thought…I had won the first Kentucky Derby I saw, but Cavalcade ran by him to spoil that. It was still the biggest thrill I ever had and the biggest disappointment — all at once, all within 20 seconds." [2]

Discovery managed one win — an allowance score — in his next four starts, then made a remarkable turnaround, winning seven of his last ten trips, including the Brooklyn Handicap, his first stakes victory. He won the ten-furlong Whitney by ten lengths and the Potomac Handicap by four lengths with 128 pounds.

In the ten-furlong Maryland Handicap at Laurel Park on October 20, Discovery revealed another dimension — speed — winning by a half-length over Good Goods in 2:03 after posting track-record split times in the preceding nine furlongs.

After losing his first five starts of 1935, Discovery rebounded to win eleven of his next fourteen outings, including eight in a row. That skein began with a thrashing of that year's Triple Crown winner, Omaha, in the Brooklyn Handicap while setting a new world record for nine furlongs in 1:48 1/5.

In the Detroit Challenge Cup on June 29, he met the seven-year-old gelding Azucar, who had won the inaugural Santa Anita Handicap earlier in the year. Arranged by Azucar's owner Fred Alger, the match race at a mile and three-sixteenths was run on a muddy track over Detroit's old Fair Grounds. Azucar carried 127 pounds to Discovery's 126, but the concession had no bearing on the outcome. Discovery broke on top and extended his lead throughout. Using a freight train parked on tracks running parallel to the backstretch, track announcer Mike Hawkins called: "Now down the backside, it's Discovery by twelve box cars." Discovery won by thirty lengths in 1:58 1/5, equaling Cavalcade's track record set the year before on a fast track.

The winning streak continued with six wins over the next five weeks, including the Stars and Stripes Handicap by six, the Butler Handicap with 132 pounds, the Bunker Hill Handicap by fifteen lengths under 131 pounds, the Arlington Handicap at ten furlongs setting a track record of 2:01 1/5 under 135 pounds, the mile Wilson Stakes by six, and the Merchants' & Citizens' Handicap on August 10. In the Merchants' & Citizens', Discovery carried 139 pounds, giving twenty-two pounds to stakes winners Stand Pat and Top Row, to lead all the way and win by two lengths.

He was second in an attempt to carry that weight again just eleven days later in the Narragansett Special, then won the Whitney Stakes, Hawthorne Gold Cup, and the Cincinnati Handicap in his remaining five outings. His two losses occurred under 138 pounds. The official year-end championships were still a year away, but very few argued that Discovery wasn't the best horse in the country. With eleven victories in nineteen starts, he won over eight different tracks in four states, and his earnings of $102,545 led all four-year-olds.

Many contended that 1936 was his best year, although he won only six of his fourteen starts. Maturing at 16.1 hands and 1,180 pounds, the "Big Train" averaged 132.4 pounds in ten of his starts and competed coast to coast on seven different tracks in five states. He won the San Carlos Handicap at Santa Anita with 130 pounds, the Inchcape Handicap at Aqueduct under 135 pounds, his third Brooklyn Handicap by four lengths under 136 pounds, the Saratoga Handicap by six lengths under 132 pounds, and the weight-for-age Wilson and Whitney Stakes by a combined eighteen lengths.

Even a train has its limits, and Discovery was finally humbled when racing secretary John B. Campbell handed him 143 pounds for the Merchants' & Citizens' Handicap on August 8. Discovery tired under his heavy impost and finished last among the five starters. He had conceded the winner forty-three pounds.

His great career ended on September 30, 1936, before a fickle crowd in the Havre de Grace Handicap in Maryland. Under 128 pounds, Discovery never fired, and finished fifth to a smattering of boos. Some of the newspaper reports the next day referred to him as a quitter. But the writers had been in such a hurry to file their stories that they failed to see Discovery walk off the track lame. "The handicappers had won their battle," noted Turf historian John Hervey wrote. "They had at length sent him from the race course not only beaten but limping, his steel-and-whipcord underpinning finally yielding…"

The undisclosed ailment wasn't serious, but Vanderbilt wisely decided that Discovery had nothing left to prove. He was Sagamore's future, not to be gambled away with a bad step in the heat of battle. He won twenty-seven of sixty-three starts, earned $195,287, and carried 130 pounds or more twenty times and won half of them. He won on any track, under any condition, and took on all comers.

Meanwhile, Vanderbilt had acquired a controlling share in Pimlico, much to the chagrin of some in the Maryland Jockey Club who thought the relative youngster was a bit too liberal. Since its founding in Annapolis in 1745, the Maryland Jockey Club had been led by Maryland's old guard and run on the strictest of regimens. George Washington was an early patron, and Andrew Jackson was known to convene Congress on occasion so that its members could attend the races. Pimlico Race Course opened in 1870, and policies voted on in the boardroom mainly affected the well-to-do. After all, they spent most of the money and purchased the luxury boxes and the high-priced Thoroughbreds. The $2 bettor was a necessary, but voiceless, part of the picture.

Vanderbilt, the youngest-ever member of The Jockey Club, brought several changes to Pimlico, such as introducing the popular Pimlico Special, won in its inaugural year in 1937 by Triple Crown champ War Admiral. Vanderbilt staged a major coup in 1938 when he brought War Admiral and Seabiscuit together in the Pimlico Special. The "Race of the Century" was won by Seabiscuit.

Other changes included installing the Puett mechanical starting gate and a public address system so everyone could follow the race's progress. A fancier of stamina, Vanderbilt created the Exterminator Handicap at about two and a quarter miles and reinstated the Pimlico Cup at two and a half miles. Not all of his changes were so well taken by the old guard, however, especially the leveling of the "mountain in the infield."

For some reason the track had been built around a fair-sized hill, and thus gained its nickname, "Old Hilltop." Those sitting in the upper sections of the grandstand could see over it to the action in the back-stretch, but the fans in the lower levels couldn't. So, Vanderbilt had it removed.

With his lean 130-pound five-foot-ten-and-a-half-inch frame and boyishly handsome face, Vanderbilt was increasingly seen in the newspapers and newrcels, and was likened to a young Jimmy Stewart. He was America's most eligible bachelor.

But not for long. In 1938, he met Manuela (Molly) Hudson in her cousin Charles S. Howard's box at Santa Anita and married her that same year.

In the meantime, Discovery was doing quite well on the farm. His first runners were a sturdy lot. His first crop, the class of 1938, included Exploration, who started 182 times, and Distant Isle, who ran 131 times. Among the 1939 crop was Lord Calvert, who raced 133 times. The next year's class included New Moon, with twenty-one victories in 102 trips. His best daughter was the hard-knocking Conniver, who won the handicap mare championship as a four-year-old in 1948 and defeated the likes of Gallorette and Stymie. Discovery's most financially productive runner was the sturdy gelding Find, a member of Sagamore's great triumvirate of 1950. He raced 110 times, won twenty-two races, and brought home part of the purse in fifty-four others for earnings of $803,615, which topped the other two members of Sagamore's top trio, stablemates Native Dancer and Social Outcast.

In 1940, Vanderbilt was asked to succeed ailing Joseph Widener as president of Belmont Park. As at Pimlico, he was concerned with the average racing fan and was often seen standing in line, rain or shine, at the $2 windows and the souvenir and food stands. When he spoke before the Thoroughbred Club of America in 1953, he said he believed that all race fans want, "is a comfortable, attractive place to see the races from, and I think they are entitled to it."

By the beginning of World War II, Vanderbilt's marriage to Molly had fallen apart. In 1942, he stepped down as president of both Belmont and Pimlico, joined the Navy, and signed up for PT-boat duty. Bud Stotler had resigned as trainer in January of 1940 due to an automobile accident the previous April. Before leaving for PT-boat training school in Rhode Island, Vanderbilt left orders that most of the racing stable be sold, keeping only the most promising runners.

The following spring found Lieutenant Vanderbilt on scouting and ambushing missions in the South Pacific Islands. He had served on forty patrols, during which he gained command of his own PT-boat. A severe tropical fungal infection in one foot sent him to the hospital, and he was certified as unfit for tropics duty. Vanderbilt was transferred to a cruiser in the Aleutians and at war's end was in a combat intelligence school in Honolulu. For his service, he was awarded the Silver Star.

Vanderbilt returned home in 1945 to find many changes, not the least being in Vanderbilt himself.

CHAPTER 3

"He'll do."

History is written on 'what ifs.' What if the *Lusitania* had sailed a day sooner, or a day later?

And what if Polynesian had been gelded when he was two?

Think of the consequences: Native Dancer would never have existed. Racing would be without two of its Triple Crown winners, Seattle Slew and Affirmed. No Raise a Native and all his descendants. Californians would not have known Native Diver. Ruffian would never have claimed our hearts and then broken them. No Cigar. No Northern Dancer.

Polynesian wasn't gelded, of course. And we have a nest of hornets to thank.

Although Polynesian stood the last part of his stud career at Gallaher Farm, his roots were deeper at Joseph Widener's Elmendorf Farm. He was foaled there on March 8, 1942, as was his sire, Unbreakable, in 1935. Grandsire Sickle, a stakes winner in England and a son of the mighty foundation sire Phalaris, was imported by Peter Widener to stand at Elmendorf.

Polynesian lost his dam, Black Polly, to colic three weeks after he was born and he was raised on cow's milk. Through Black Polly, he traced back to the superb Black Toney mare Black Maria. Black Toney also sired Bimelech and the 1924 Kentucky Derby winner Black Gold.

When Joseph Widener died in 1943, Elmendorf passed to his son, Peter A. B. Widener II. Not long afterward, Widener asked the farm's trainer, Morris Dixon, to pick a promising individual from the yearling crop that he could give his wife, Gertrude, for their upcoming anniversary. Dixon chose Polynesian. Another source mentions it was a Christmas gift, but in any case, Mrs. Widener grew very fond of the brown colt.

Polynesian was sent to High Tor, Morris Dixon's training farm near Newton Square, Pennsylvania, for his tutoring. Dixon, a former amateur hunt rider, had trained steeplechasers first and still handled jumpers on occasion. Although Polynesian was to race on the flat,

Dixon taught him to jump as well. Bad idea. The colt went through his career happily dumping his riders whenever the urge hit him to go over a fence — as Turf journalist Joe Palmer put it, "…just for the hell of it." [1]

The incident with the hornets occurred during his juvenile campaign in 1944.

Polynesian debuted on April 23, 1944. In his first three starts, he had two thirds and a fourth before bucked shins put him on the sidelines. The bizarre story began after he resumed training at Delaware Park and grew ill following a brisk workout. At first it was thought he had "tied up," a condition that usually follows a hard work or a race when the muscles stiffen badly as the bloodstream fails to rid itself of waste. It turned out, however, that Polynesian was suffering from a toxic blood poisoning that partially paralyzed his hindquarters and caused some hair loss.

He was a pitiful sight when he arrived at High Tor to recover. This once-handsome colt with large patches of bare skin had to be half-carried from the van to his stall. Through June and into July, he gradually recovered. But now he suffered from 'psychosomatic trauma.'

"He wouldn't move if he could help it," Dixon

recalled. "We had to haul him out of the stall in the morning, and when we got him to the paddock, he'd just stand there...Then at night we had to haul him back in." [2]

Polynesian, who had learned that movement caused pain, refused to move any more than necessary. In his paddock, he ambled over to the shade of a tree, where he would graze, or just lean against the trunk.

The veterinarian offered Gertrude Widener two options: bleed him with leeches or geld him. A third choice would have to be considered if all else failed. Then one day, providence intervened.

Polynesian was standing under his tree as usual, and keeping him company was Dixon's young son. Hornets had built a nest in that tree and, well, you get the picture.

Dixon was in his bedroom changing clothes when his son shouted that "Polynesian was going crazy, running around the field." Asked what happened, the boy explained that Polynesian was rolling in the dirt and hit the tree. The hornets emerged and attacked the biggest target they could find. "They hit him everywhere," Dixon said, "and he just ran and ran and ran.

It had taken four men to load him. Now it took four men to catch him." [3]

The story didn't end there. He recovered from the stings, returned to the racetrack in mid-August, and ran as if the hornets were still after him, winning five of his seven remaining starts that year, including the Sagamore Stakes at Laurel. "He was never right," Dixon recalled. "He was always a little stiff...I never let 'Gertie' Widener see him unless I had him walk around the back of the barn to get his soreness out." [4]

Now he had another hangup — he hated to train, and if he was kept at any track too long, he refused to run. Most trainers might have given up by now, but Dixon knew the colt had talent, and somewhere inside that mixed-up head was a desire to compete. So he took his time with him and backed off when needed. But without proper conditioning, Polynesian never developed enough "bottom" to win beyond nine furlongs.

Still, he was a genuine racehorse, winning the 1945 Preakness over Kentucky Derby winner Hoop, Jr. and the Withers Stakes over previously unbeaten Pavot. He was champion sprinter in 1947. He retired to Elmendorf with a record of twenty-seven wins — sixteen of them stakes — in fifty-eight starts, with twenty placings for $310,410 in earnings. He broke or equaled six track records and one world record, won twice with 134 pounds, and never ducked an opponent.

Moved to Gallaher Farm in 1948 when Peter Widener died, Polynesian sired only thirty-seven stakes winners, but his influence transcends generations. His daughter Alanesian, who, when bred to the prepotent Bold Ruler, got Boldnesian, grandsire of Triple Crown winner Seattle Slew. His son Imbros, a good runner in his own right, produced the California idol Native Diver, who won at distances from four furlongs to a mile and five-eighths. In 1956, according to *The Thoroughbred Record Stallion Register*, Polynesian became the first stallion since Star Shoot in 1916 to sire six juvenile stakes winners in a single season. Polynesian died on December 29, 1959 at age seventeen from a twisted intestine. By then his fame as a sire had been etched in stone, if only for the gray colt that was born in 1950 just across the road from Gallaher.

The hornets' nest at High Tor should have been preserved so it could someday accompany Polynesian to the Racing Hall of Fame.

"All I know about breeding can be said in a minute or two. If you breed a mare of ability to a stallion of ability, you've got a better chance of getting a horse of ability than if you don't. In other words, if you want to breed better horses, get better mares or better stallions or, better still, get both."

Whether or not Alfred Vanderbilt meant to coin a new tongue-twisting slogan for breeding, by the early 1950s he had more good stakes winners coming out of Sagamore than the New York Yankees had winning pennants. And to think, just a few years earlier he had all but given up on racing.

Like many veterans coming home in 1945, Vanderbilt returned with a different perspective on life. He became more involved in charities, particularly those dealing with war veterans. His divorce from second wife, Jeanne Murray, was final. And Miyako, the mare in whom he had placed much hope, had died after producing only three foals, all by Discovery.

He had purchased the daughter of John P. Grier—La Chica in 1940 because he liked her potential as a broodmare. Her three foals were a non-stakes-winning gelding, a steeplechaser, and the roan filly named Geisha.

Geisha was a little thing, a trait that manifested itself for each of three generations back to Sweep. Ralph Kercheval remembers her as a "nice little, round, short mare. She was very pleasant looking, very feminine, and was pretty true leg-wise." Geisha launched her racing career soon after Vanderbilt returned home, running second in her debut. She raced twice more that year, without winning, and broke her maiden at Santa Anita early in 1946, her only victory in eleven career starts, with earnings of $4,120.

With Stotler retired and Vanderbilt concentrating his energies elsewhere, Sagamore's slump hit bottom in 1948 when the stable ranked number twenty-eight among money-winning owners. Then, as Vanderbilt watched some of Discovery's yearlings breezing on the farm's training track, he recalled the exhilaration he had felt when Discovery led Cavalcade to the top of the stretch of the 1934 Kentucky Derby, and he decided he needn't abandon racing to work for his charities. He hired a new full-time trainer, William C. Winfrey, and Kercheval to manage his farm.

In 1949, Bed o' Roses, a bay granddaughter of Discovery, galloped through a season that led her to the two-year-old filly championship. And in 1950, Next Move, a Bull Lea filly out of Vanderbilt's mare Now What, smashed just about everything on her way to the three-year-old filly championship.

Geisha was first bred to Questionnaire, getting the winning filly Orientation. Then in 1949, she was sent to Polynesian's court at Gallaher Farm in Lexington, Kentucky. Wrote Joe Hirsch of the *Daily Racing Form*: "The result of that tryst was a gray colt with a striking presence, ability and style." [5]

Kercheval, in charge of Sagamore's breeding program, had recommended the mating. When asked why a mare with a family of short speed was bred to a stallion who never won at more than nine furlongs, Kercheval replied, "We liked Polynesian for his brilliance. There might be horses who could run two, three days, but they wouldn't have the brilliance. The brilliance and the speed was what we were looking for."

Another of Kercheval's jobs was to break the yearlings, and he said he had no trouble breaking Discovery's big gray grandson. "He impressed me as an extremely nice colt," said Kercheval. "From the word 'go' he was on the ball. And he was smart. He reacted exactly as you'd want him to. He had everything you'd want if you were to pick out a good horse."

Vanderbilt was well known for the names he gave his horses. Social Outcast was a favorite example, his name a play on words from his parentage, Shut Out—Pansy, and the fact that Vanderbilt had been dropped from the social register after marrying his second wife, Jeanne Murray. But Vanderbilt often expressed regret over the name he gave the son of Polynesian and Geisha.

"If I had to do it over again," he said many times, "I'd probably done a better job...A lot of people think Native Dancer is a filly."

On a cool, misty morning at Santa Anita in December of 1951, Vanderbilt and Winfrey hoped to see if any of the yearlings had the qualities of brilliance and speed that Kercheval had envisioned in the mating of Geisha and Polynesian. Winfrey clocked the big gray colt, working with three other yearlings, in :23 flat for a quarter mile. The colt hadn't worked up a sweat. Three days later, a *Daily Racing Form* clocker stopped him in :23 1/5. Again, not a hair was turned.

Alfred Vanderbilt nodded. "He'll do."

CHAPTER 4

"...all the earmarks of a champion."

Following Native Dancer's December workouts, Bill Winfrey advised waiting until the Jamaica meeting in April to start him.

The trainer knew the gray colt had class, but he had been in the business long enough to know not to let one's expectations get too high. Winfrey, at age thirty-six, had learned that lesson well with other horses, and he had two in the barn for Vanderbilt — the frustrating Cousin, a top two-year-old in 1951 before he suddenly decided he didn't want to run anymore, and the delicate Crash Dive — who weren't making life easy for their trainer.

"(Crash Dive) was to have been the big horse from the 1950 crop," Winfrey said years later. "But he had soundness problems and was hard to keep in training."

Among these "problem" horses, Native Dancer

seemed too good to be true. "He did whatever I wanted him to," Winfrey said. "If I wanted a fast work, he'd give me a fast work. If I just wanted a gallop, he would do that."

By the time the gray colt debuted at Jamaica on April 19, 1952, the fans had heard about his workouts and sent the colt, bearing tattoo number F6888, to the gate as the 7-5 favorite. Jamaica, now long gone, was a singular course anomalous to America's fixation with ovals. No two sides were alike: the 1,062-foot backstretch was 124-feet longer than the front, and the sweeping far turn of 2,008 feet was a full 860 feet longer than its counterpart. It made for interesting strategies on a jockey's part.

Native Dancer's rider was Eric Guerin, a twenty-eight-year-old native of Maringuoin, Louisiana. Years later, Guerin recalled that the colt was "flighty" and jumped shadows all down the backstretch. But when he asked the colt to run, Guerin said he'd "never felt that kind of power." Winning by four and a half lengths in :59 3/5, Native Dancer stole the thunder from the card's headliner, the Wood Memorial, in which Master Fiddle beat the 1951 juvenile champion Tom Fool.

Native Dancer paid $4.80 for a $2 win ticket; never again would he go off at less than odds-on.

On a drizzly Wednesday four days later, 22,954 fans sent him off at 4-5 over eleven rivals in Jamaica's Youthful Stakes. Guerin allowed the gray to run just off the early pace, then pushed a button, and Native Dancer, in the words of *The Morning Telegraph*'s Fred Galiani, "just exploded at the top of the stretch...and loped on to a six-length victory...although it is a bit early to say he is the best, the Polynesian colt has all the earmarks of a champion." [1]

Immediately afterward, Winfrey boarded a plane for Louisville, Kentucky, where he tried to coax Cousin to run in the Derby Trial. "Cousin is the Vanderbilt 3-year-old that considers horse racing a sinful occupation," Red Smith jested in the *New York Herald Tribune*. "Vanderbilt and Winfrey pleaded with Cousin to win the Kentucky Derby this year, but he said the hell with it and went off to sulk on Sagamore Farm in Maryland."

Cousin never made it to the Derby; he was scratched after his "the hell-with-it" attitude in the Trial.

Winfrey returned to New York to more bad news. Native Dancer had bucked shins, an inflammation common in young horses subjecting underdeveloped bones and joints to stress. Nothing serious, but he would be out of action for awhile.

Native Dancer made his return that August at Saratoga, the venerable upstate New York racetrack.

The community of Saratoga Springs was established in 1773 and named after an Iroquois word, "Sarachtogoe." Its spring waters had been known to the area's native peoples long before being "discovered" by the Europeans in 1643.

In 1863, John "Old Smoke" Morrissey, a gambler, boxing champion, and future congressman, built a racecourse in Saratoga Springs, called it Horse Haven, and held a three-day mixed meet of Thoroughbred and trotting races. Its success stirred Morrissey and three partners, William Travers, Leonard Jerome, and John Hunter, to build a larger facility on 125 acres across Union Avenue. Saratoga Racecourse, under the Saratoga Association, opened on August 2, 1864, with 10,000 spectators on hand. Travers, the first president, owned Kentucky, winner of the inaugural Travers Stakes.

Affluent New Yorkers flocked to the Adirondacks, watched the races at Saratoga, reveled in the splendor of the Grand Union Hotel, and energized in the mineral springs. Saratoga continues its old-fashioned ways each August.

In 1952, old Saratoga witnessed a phenomenon when Native Dancer swept the Flash, Saratoga Special, Grand Union Hotel, and Hopeful Stakes from August 4 to August 30. No juvenile had ever won as many as four of Saratoga's two-year-old events in so short a time.

Beginning with the Flash, the 4-5 favorite beat a good field by two and a quarter lengths after being carried wide on the turn by Greentree Stable's well-regarded Tiger Skin, the 2-1 second choice. Twelve days later, he won the six-furlong Saratoga Special over a sloppy track, defeating Tahiti, a Polynesian colt unbeaten in two starts. The Dancer handled the off track like he had four-wheel drive, which Guerin used to his advantage by saving ground along the rail.

Of his four rivals in the Grand Union Hotel Stakes a week later, two were multiple stakes winners: Tahitian King, yet another unbeaten son of Polynesian coming in off four straight victories, and Trio Stable's Laffango, who had three consecutive scores. Native Dancer carried 126 pounds, four over the scale, and conceded from four to twelve pounds to his opponents. The fans sent the gray off at 1-2, with Tahitian King and Laffango the second and third picks. The Dancer stalked their pace for four furlongs, then advanced to an early lead, and drew out to win by three and a half lengths in 1:11 1/5, the best six furlongs of the meeting.

More than 24,000 fans came out on August 30, the meet's last day, to watch him win the Hopeful Stakes at 1-4. His self-confidence growing, Native Dancer lagged farther behind than usual, loafed once he had the lead, but easily won by two lengths. Guerin beamed afterward. "I never had a second of worry. He took off when I asked him to. On the way back to unsaddle, I told Ted Atkinson that he'd have to ride him to see just how good he is." The Hopeful's purse, $51,450, nearly doubled his previous earnings of $54,425.

After four races in twenty-six days, The Dancer was rested until September 22, when he won the six-furlong Anticipation Purse, a prep for the Futurity at Belmont Park, as well as, an introduction to the straight Widener Course. He beat Tahitian King by only one and a quarter lengths, but had a great deal more in the tank had he needed it. Five days later, he did.

Joseph Widener installed the course named for him in 1925. Vanderbilt had wanted it discontinued when he was Belmont president in 1940. He contended that only the wealthier patrons in the grandstands' upper decks could see the early part of a race. The seven-furlong course began out in the hinterlands northeast of the grandstand and ran southwest, twice bisected the training oval, entered the main track near where turn two enters the backstretch, and ended where it entered the main track across from the clubhouse.

Worth $82,845 to the winner, the Futurity was the marquee race for two-year-olds in the East, and, according to Joe A. Estes, the longtime editor of *The Blood-Horse*, in *American Race Horses of 1952*, was "one of the most difficult races in America for anything but a top-class horse to win..."

The crowd of 40,556 picked Tahitian King as the strong second choice with Cain Hoy Stable's Dark Star the third pick on the basis of three wins, including the Juvenile Stakes, in four outings. In spite of rumors that his right ankle was noticeably large, Native Dancer was bet down to 1-3. As for the ankle, Bob Horwood of *The Morning Telegraph* wrote that it "had looked 'suspicious' for some weeks but had never caused the colt to take a lame step." [2]

Little Request blistered the opening quarter in :21 4/5, before hitting empty. Jockey Eddie Arcaro maneuvered Tahitian King to the outside and stopped the clock at six furlongs in 1:08 2/5, just a tick off the track record. Guerin aimed for the same path, but found it closed by tiring horses. He then spotted a small fluctuating hole between horses and gunned the gray through. They were in the clear, but not in the lead. Tahitian King was still more than two lengths ahead.

With that surge of power Joe Hirsch described as a "fearsome acceleration," the gray blew by and drew off to win by two and a quarter lengths in 1:14 2/5, equaling Porter's Mite's world record for a straight course. Never threatened with the whip, Native Dancer ran the final half-furlong in six seconds. "Native Dancer had tremendous speed," Winfrey said years later. "But I trained him to rate."

"He never has done anything wrong," said Winfrey after the race. "He comes back from his races playing with the groom, has a voracious appetite, and never appears to lose his poise and confidence." Winfrey

admitted wishing the colt would do "some little incon-
sequential thing wrong just to reassure he is a horse." [3]
Soon afterward, the Dancer ditched Bernie Everson, his
exercise rider, and did so with some regularity after
that, as if to reassure his trainer that no matter how
famous he became, he was still just a horse at heart.

Winfrey had planned to end the Dancer's season after
the Futurity, but to silence the stamina skeptics, the colt
went to the post for the East View Stakes at Jamaica on
October 22. A mile and one-sixteenth was as far as juveniles were asked to go in the United States, and it also
would be Native Dancer's first time around two turns.
The 1-5 choice came from far back to beat the
Champagne Stakes winner, Laffango, by a length and a
half in 1:44 1/5. The first prize of $38,525 boosted his
earnings to $230,495, supplanting Top Flight's previous
juvenile earnings record of $219,000. The gray was sent
to Sagamore for some rest and relaxation before joining
Winfrey in California sometime over the winter.

Shortly after Native Dancer joined the stable at
Santa Anita, his ankles were fired for osselets, a bony
growth at the joint. "Just a precaution," Winfrey said as
he attempted to stifle rumors the gray wasn't sound.

"Better now than next spring wishing we had."

The *Daily Racing Form*'s Charles Hatton believed there was an ankle problem. "It would be surprising if they did not eventually show some indication of wear and tear," he wrote. "For very fast horses usually 'go' first in the ankles, and he is about as fast as horses ever become." [4]

Toward late November, attention turned to the year-end championships, including Horse of the Year. Back in August after Native Dancer swept Saratoga, the talk had started. Some thought the idea of naming any two-year-old as Horse of the Year bordered on the profane. It had never happened. Not with Bimelech. Not even Citation or Count Fleet.

Official voting for championships began in 1936, and through 1949 were decided by writers and handicappers of the *Turf and Sport Digest* and the *Daily Racing Form/Morning Telelgraph*. In 1950, they were joined by the racing secretaries and handicappers of the country's major tracks, under the Thoroughbred Racing Associations (TRA), which had voted for its own champions. (Beginning in 1971, the voting was consolidated into the Eclipse Awards.) The three groups had generally concurred in their decisions, one being that two-year-olds just aren't awarded Horse of the Year.

Besides there were plenty of top three-year-olds and older runners with championship-caliber seasons, including Tom Fool, the 1951 juvenile champion; Calumet Farm's Hill Gail, unprecedented winner of the Santa Anita and Kentucky Derbys and the Derby Trial; and One Count, a son of Count Fleet, winner of four of his last five starts, two against older horses, at distances from ten to sixteen furlongs.

The suspense ended in late November when both the *Turf and Sport Digest* and the TRA voted for Native Dancer, while the *Daily Racing Form/Morning Telegraph* picked One Count. Of the latter, Hatton wrote, "...Horse of the Year honors are not for leaders of certain age or sex divisions when the candidates include a classic winner such as One Count. He answered in the affirmative questions of stamina, weight carrying ability and versatility the owners of two-year-olds can only hope they will answer as satisfactorily." [5]

John B. Campbell, longtime handicapper for the New York tracks, ranked him with 130 pounds to top the Experimental Free Handicap. Laffango and Tahitian

King were next with 123. Since Walter S. Vosburgh began compiling the year-end rankings in 1933, only three juveniles had been ranked with 130 pounds or more: Bimelech in 1939, Alsab in 1941, and Count Fleet, at 132 pounds, in 1942. The seven-pound spread between The Dancer and the next two was the biggest since the ratings began. Len Tracy blasted those who knocked the quality of the 1952 juvenile crop. "Regardless of Native Dancer's prowess," he wrote in *The Thoroughbred Record*, "Laffango and other juveniles need no apologies when judged on their own."

Laffango won six of eleven starts, including divisions of the Tyro and Sapling Stakes, and the Champagne and Garden State Stakes, with two seconds to Native Dancer. Tahitian King won the National Stallion and the U.S. Hotel Stakes, and also was second twice to the gray. Then there was Straight Face, who despite a bad knee and a sour temper for which he was gelded, won the Breeders' Futurity and Jockey Club Stakes.

And so the year ended much as it began, with a buzz of anticipation. "It will be interesting to note," Hatton wrote, "what sort Native Dancer proves at three. Indeed this is one of the fascinations of the 1952 season." [6]

NATIVE DANCER

CHAPTER 5

The Road To Louisville

ative Dancer's road to Louisville nearly ended in January of 1953 at Santa Anita.

He was on his way to the track for a workout with Bernie Everson up, when an irresistible horse urge came over him. He ditched Everson and took off on a high-spirited tour of Santa Anita. He plowed through flower beds and jumped fences. Happy as a school kid on a Friday afternoon, Native Dancer reveled in his freedom for ten minutes before he stepped on a rein, pulled himself up, and allowed himself to be caught.

The horse was fine. But Bill Winfrey felt ten years older. "He needs a good hard race," he told a friend as he wiped perspiration from his face.

Even the slightest bump on one of those ankles would have compromised a Derby schedule that called for the colt to go six furlongs in March. Those ankles drove Winfrey to distraction. They had been fairly large prior to the Flash Stakes the previous year; his right fore had been pretty big before the colt's world-record-equaling run in the Futurity. That same ankle had developed some heat in it prior to the East View, but the colt had never taken a bad step.

In handling a horse like Native Dancer, Winfrey's emotions ran the gamut. Blessed, certainly; even apprehensive. And guilty. "My dad has worked hard all his life and never had a horse like this one," he would tell reporters over the next two years. He was even more specific when Turf writer John McNulty visited the trainer and Native Dancer at Belmont Park prior to the colt's public workout. McNulty had extended his hand and called him "Mister Winfrey."

"I'm Bill Winfrey," the trainer corrected. "Mister Winfrey is a trainer over at Jamaica. He's my father." He told McNulty that any number of men had been training for fifty years or more without ever getting a horse like this one. "Tell the truth, a man of thirty-seven doesn't deserve it, that's all." [1]

Bill Winfrey was correct in that his sixty-eight-year-old father, Carey Winfrey, never saddled a horse close to The Dancer's caliber; but he accomplished enough to merit induction into the Racing Hall of Fame in 1975, four years after his son. The best horse the Texas-born trainer ever handled was Dedicate, the handicap champion of 1957.

William Colin Winfrey was born Colin Dickard in Detroit in 1915. His father died when Bill was about four. After his mother married Carey Winfrey two or three years later, Bill was adopted and never referred to Carey as anything but his father. Carey's home base was Aqueduct and that was where Bill grew up. When he wasn't following the race meetings with his father, he attended grammar school P.S. 108, just across the street from Aqueduct; no doubt making it difficult for the boy to concentrate. He dropped out of John Adams High School after convincing his parents he wanted to work for his father. Bill started by "walking hots." He acquired his jockey's license when he was sixteen, his weight grounding him soon after, and his trainer's license two years later. His first stakes winner was Postage Due in 1938.

Bill served in the Marines during World War II and was operating his own public stable in 1949 when he was hired in early spring by Vanderbilt. That year, he

sent Bed o' Roses to a juvenile filly championship. In
1950, he conditioned Next Move to the three-year-old
filly championship, then Bed o' Roses to the handicap
mare championship the following year. And now, this
big gray seemed hell-bent on turning Winfrey's already
thinning hair the same color as his own.

On Saturday, February 7, Native Dancer appeared
before 47,500 fans at Santa Anita. He only jogged, but
the fans loved it. Eleven days later, he turned three furlongs in :39, and on February 21, posted the same distance in :37 1/5. On March 13, he went seven furlongs
in 1:28, and the next day Winfrey put him on a train
for New York.

The road to Louisville had begun.

On a wet and bone-chilling first day of spring, two
days after arriving at Belmont, Native Dancer limbered
up with a two-mile gallop on Belmont's training track
before a host of news media. Having put on about a
hundred pounds that filled in the lanky juvenile spots
and standing 16.1 hands, he definitely impressed
everyone who hadn't seen him since the East View.

Charles Hatton, with *The Morning Telegraph*, wrote
that the colt had "improved extraordinarily from two to

three…he emerged well balanced, appearing more 'of a piece' as turfmen say." [2]

John McNulty found the colt majestic enough "…to be looked at for a long, long while…and often. He was tuned so exquisitely he almost thrummed standing still." [3]

Turf writer George F. T. Ryall tempered his admiration with reality. It was late March and the colt hadn't raced in five months. Most of the top Derby hopefuls already had nine-furlong efforts behind them, including Straight Face, who won the Flamingo back in February. Royal Bay Gem had gone the distance twice. Money Broker won the Florida Derby later in the same day as Dancer's gallop.

"…it seems to me," Ryall wrote in *The Blood-Horse*, "that he is going to have a lot to do, and not a great deal of time to do it in, between now and the first Saturday in May…if he coughs; or runs even a little temperature…or shows any ill effects after a race or a work, the whole carefully planned routine can be tossed out the window."

Two days later, Native Dancer breezed five furlongs in 1:02 3/5. Then on April 4, he went a mile in 1:41

1/5. And four days later, he knocked the time down to 1:39 over a muddy surface. Winfrey thought he was ready for competition and entered him in the six-furlong Assault Purse at Jamaica on Monday, April 13. But Jamaica officials canceled the race when only two other horses were entered. Fans who had skipped work to see him were furious. Vanderbilt and Winfrey were more than angry, and the officials agreed to a public workout following the fifth race the next day. Still, a workout is a workout, not a race.

Oscar Fraley, staff writer for the United Press, understood. In an article apearing in the April 14 *Louisville Times*, he wrote that Native Dancer "has a lot of work cut out for him in the next few weeks" and would be practically "cold" when he started in the Gotham Stakes on Saturday, April 18.

The next afternoon, The Dancer and two stablemates were vanned to Jamaica from Belmont. Following the fifth race, race caller Fred L. Capossela announced Native Dancer's entry onto the track, resulting in a mass movement of fans from the lines at the mutuel windows, food stands, and elsewhere, to the rail or their seats. Cheers greeted the gray and his running mates, six-year-old First Glance, a good hand-icap-winning son of Discovery, and Beachcomber, an unraced three-year-old with exercise rider Albert Bao on board. Bernie Everson rode First Glance, and Eric Guerin was glad to be back on The Dancer.

The plan was for Beachcomber, who had speed but burned out early, to take the lead. Guerin would keep Native Dancer six or eight lengths behind until the stretch, where Everson would bring First Glance up to challenge, thereby giving The Dancer a target to run at and a challenge from behind.

Breaking from the starting gate set up at the six-fur-long pole, Native Dancer nearly pulled Guerin out of the saddle to take the lead. Beachcomber never made it anywhere close to where he was supposed to be, and Guerin had to strangle his mount in order for First Glance to catch up. The Dancer's time was a moderate 1:14, but he was under the hardest of holds.

The trial, which the media dubbed the "Winfrey Purse," didn't impress some observers. With the Derby less than three weeks away, there was concern that Winfrey was over-cautious with those ankles and was bringing him along too slowly. Some writers didn't even like the way he walked off the track, which rankled Vanderbilt to no end. "It was a good workout to me...how can you fault it when he wasn't set down for speed...?" [4]

Meanwhile, other Derby hopefuls continued to move along in their preparations. Eugene Constantin Jr.'s heavily campaigned Royal Bay Gem won the Chesapeake Stakes at Bowie on April 11. When George Krehbiel of the *Detroit News* heard the results, he turned to his fellow workers and declared, "There's your Derby winner, boys, and I don't care how many gray horses they send down from New York." [5] The Chesapeake was the thirtieth start and the eighth just that year for the son of imported Royal Gem II. He previously had won the Everglades at nine furlongs and finished a fast-closing second to Straight Face in the Flamingo.

Even more impressive was Correspondent's win in the Blue Grass Stakes at Keeneland on April 23. The California-bred colt, owned by Mrs. Gordon Guilberson and trained by Wally Dunn, broke his maiden in his third start of the year. After three more starts, including a third in the Santa Anita Derby, he won an overnight handicap. He went on to Keeneland where he won an allowance on April 10, going six furlongs in 1:11 1/5. A week later, with Eddie Arcaro aboard, he set Keeneland's railbirds to buzzing with a win at seven furlongs in 1:23, the second fastest ever at the track.

In the Blue Grass, the son of imported Khaled proved he could turn on the afterburners more than once. After gaining the lead, Arcaro allowed Straight Face to pull within striking distance, then set Correspondent down for the drive. Winning by five lengths, Correspondent's final time for the nine furlongs, 1:49, took a tick off of Coaltown's track record.

Meanwhile The Dancer turned a lot of heads himself when he hung up a :46 3/5 for a half-mile. This came on the afternoon of Friday, April 17, the day before he faced a starter for the first time in five months in the inaugural Gotham Stakes at Jamaica. Eighteen entries forced the track to split the race into two divisions. The gray drew the first division, while his stiffest competition, Laffango and Invigorator, ran in the second. The 38,201 fans sent him off at 1-6, the shortest odds of his career to this point.

Shown on national television, Native Dancer's win brought a legion of new fans to the sport, including this writer. He won in a steady, businesslike manner, running the mile and one-sixteenth in 1:44 1/5. Laffango won the second division a fifth of a second faster, but The Dancer put on a show for his television audience by jumping some footprints leading to the infield.

Some observers mistook the gray's easing up once in the lead as trouble shaking Magic Lamp. The race chart, however, indicates nothing of the kind, only that he won "ridden out." When he was passed by the two horses going into the turn, he was "still under restraint," and then "moved strongly on the outside of the early leaders nearing the stretch turn" where he was forced wide. After taking the lead in mid-stretch he "increased his margin thereafter under hand riding." [6]

After seeing the Gotham, Gayle Talbot of the Associated Press said he had a better "understanding of some of the semi-hysterical pieces we had read about him...Speaking as a new and highly enthusiastic member of the Native Dancer Marching Society, we feel he will survive both the added distance and the stronger competition and rack up No. 11 [in the Wood Memorial]."

On the Monday following the Gotham, a report reached New York from an unidentified source on the West Coast that Native Dancer was so sore he wouldn't be starting in the Wood Memorial on Saturday. It might have come from remarks made by some unidentified observers who said he appeared to "cord up" in the winner's circle.

Whether the 40,000-plus fans who jammed into Jamaica on April 25 heard the report or not, they backed the colt in record numbers. The windows closed on the Native Dancer/Social Outcast entry at 1-10 in the nationally televised race. The field, all carrying 126 pounds, included Tahitian King, Invigorator, and Spring Hill Farm's Jamie K. Eddie Arcaro was aboard Social Outcast, but he made it known that the son of Shut Out would have to throw in a huge effort to take him off Correspondent for the Derby.

The Dancer proved the reports were wrong and ran more alertly than he had in the Gotham. Stalking Tahitian King's leisurely pace, the first quarter in :24 3/5 and the half in :50, Guerin had such a lap full of horse running in second place that he was confident he could push the button anytime. When Magic Lamp came up from nowhere to put a head in front of the gray at the half, Guerin pushed the button. Native Dancer handled Tahitian King with ease and steadily drew off to win by four and a half lengths. The $87,000 purse boosted his earnings to $341,995.

As usual, the naysayers criticized his time, 1:50 3/5 on a fast track, which didn't compare with Correspondent's 1:49 in the Blue Grass. But the gray was carrying five pounds more, and as George Ryall pointed out, he ran faster third and fourth quarters than Correspondent and had a final furlong that matched Coaltown's time.

At least the Wood solved Arcaro's Derby ride situation when Social Outcast finished fourth and Vanderbilt released him from his oral agreement.

On Sunday, April 26, Winfrey loaded Native Dancer onto a Pennsylvania Limited rail car for the last leg of the road to Louisville. He had first thought to send the gray by van, but decided the train was faster and less stressful.

CHAPTER 6

"...running for the sheer joy of exercise."

Bill Winfrey couldn't sleep.

As Pennsylvania Railroad's Cincinnati Limited sped through the night, Winfrey tossed and turned in bed for three hours before giving up. He rose, dressed, turned on a night light, and opened a mystery novel. He read past midnight and into the early morning, but couldn't concentrate. His mind kept wandering to The Dancer.

Elaine Winfrey couldn't sleep either. She was concerned over her husband's fretting, true, but the light was keeping her awake. "I could have hit him," she said.[1]

The Winfreys had a room in the sleeper car, several cars behind the one carrying the horses. Bill Winfrey knew Native Dancer was okay. Les Murray and Hal Walker were with him. *And The Dancer's a good traveler*, he thought to himself.

Winfrey wasn't really sure what bothered him.

There was the stress associated with the Kentucky Derby; something he wasn't exactly a stranger to, what with the attempt to get Cousin there last year. And he had saddled Swain in 1941, substituting for the horse's trainer, who couldn't make it. Swain wasn't expected to do much and he didn't. As for The Dancer, Winfrey knew he could get ten furlongs, but had he done everything he could to get the gray fit?

No one in the media could agree on anything. Native Dancer's win in the Gotham was dull; it was spectacular. His ankles were too big; his ankles were fine. Winfrey's being too cautious with him; Winfrey's working him too hard. True, those ankles had caused many a sleepless night, but the colt had never taken a bad step.

But for tonight anyway, Native Dancer was getting a darn sight more rest than his trainer. Nothing had been overlooked to assure his comfort and safety. Since this was only an overnight jaunt, The Dancer's stall was partitioned into two sections. He was in one, and Social Outcast was in the other. Both sections were padded with bales of hay. Two broad, felt-covered shanks tethered the horses, and each wore leather headgear to protect against mild to moderate blows.

Sharing the car with The Dancer and Social Outcast were Winfrey's lead pony, Rusty; Saxon Stable's Invigorator and his groom; Winfrey's fat old fox terrier, Susie; and grooms Lester Murray and Harold Walker. The night had grown chilly. Murray put a blanket on the gray, as he likely did his stall mate and Rusty.

Departing New York City on Sunday, the Limited's route took it over Pennsylvania's mountains, into eastern Ohio to Columbus, then southwest to Cincinnati, where it would be coupled to an L&N-line train on the last leg to Louisville.

Around 4 a.m., outside of Columbus, there was a long blast of the engine's whistle followed by the sound of grinding brakes and the cars jerking to a hard stop.

Four of the country's top sports writers had been sleeping in the Pullman car — Red Smith of the *New York Herald Tribune*; Frank Graham, *New York Journal American*; Jim Roach, *The New York Times*; and Joe Williams, *New York World Telegram and Sun*. At least one was thrown from his berth and complained of hurting a rib. Farther to the rear, Winfrey dropped his book and, according to Mrs. Winfrey, shrieked, "My God, the horse!" He dashed into the aisle, where he met a porter, who explained there was a stalled vehicle on the tracks. Winfrey hopped to the roadbed and ran ahead to the car carrying the horses.

"He's all right," Les Murray told him. "He was sound asleep when it happened." Winfrey ran a hand over the colt from head to hindquarters and down the bandaged legs to the ankles. Finding nothing, he heaved a sigh of relief. Maybe this was the Derby week bugaboo.

As the train got underway again, Bill Winfrey finally got some sleep.

The rest of the journey passed without further incident, and the train arrived in Louisville around noon. Here Winfrey boarded the rail car, which was hooked to a switch engine that pulled it to a railroad siding three blocks from Churchill Downs. A large crowd of reporters and cameramen waited as the engine eased its valuable cargo to a stop next to an elevated platform. Movie cameras representing the national television networks and local stations began rolling before the train stopped. Scores of fans, adults, and kids skipping school jostled for a place from which they might get a glimpse of their hero.

After what seemed an eternity, the door opened.

Bill Winfrey stepped down and shook hands with Tom Young, Churchill Downs' track superintendent. A heavy plank was laid across the foot-long gap to the platform, then covered with a thick layer of straw and banked on either side with hay bales. Finally, Harold Walker led the colt onto the platform with Les Murray holding his tail. "It's him!" cried a boy sitting on a fence. As if on cue, the colt stopped to look over his surroundings.

He had grown into a striking animal. His head suggested strength rather than the elegance of his Arabian ancestry. His eyes blazed with the look of an eagle on the hunt. Dan Scott, who had seen both the foal and the adult Native Dancer, thought he "...was impressive to look right in the eye. He even seemed to be thinking."

Tom Young had been meeting the Kentucky Derby "celebrities" for forty-two years — War Admiral, Gallant Fox, Count Fleet, Citation, Whirlaway. But after seeing Native Dancer, he said only Twenty Grand in 1931 looked as much a Derby champion. It was an opinion echoed by Jerry McNerney of the *Louisville Courier-Journal*. "I've watched about 20 Derby winners [arrive] in Louisville," he wrote, "including Count

Fleet, Citation and Whirlaway. None gave the impression of such sheer power and bubbling over energy, as this big gray..."

Harold Walker, the Vanderbilt stable's head groom, led the colt for the cameramen, but it was Les Murray the reporters went to for a story. "I've been with this hoss most all his life," he said. "Only we turn him over to that big man [Walker] when there's a crowd around. He's bigger and can hold him down better." Regarding the train incident, Murray said, "Good thing he had that hat on. He got bumped plenty...I thought sure we had a wreck." [2]

On Tuesday morning, Native Dancer limbered up on the track with a ten minute walk around the mile oval and then jogged another mile in five minutes. Surrounded by reporters, Winfrey said he planned to breeze him and Social Outcast six furlongs on Thursday.

Derby Week got under way for real Tuesday afternoon with the sixteenth running of the Derby Trial, which had produced only two Kentucky Derby winners: Citation in 1948 and Hill Gail the previous year. Royal Bay Gem was the slight favorite over G&G Stable's Money Broker, the Florida Derby winner, in the field of fourteen. But it was the fourth betting choice, Harry Guggenheim's Dark Star, with Henry Moreno on board, who ran off to win by four lengths in 1:36, only three ticks off of Hill Gail's stakes record. Winfrey had passed on the Trial for Native Dancer because the Wood suited his colt's schedule better.

The Trial was Dark Star's first win beyond seven furlongs, although his pedigree suggested he could run all afternoon. Racing for Harry Guggenheim's Cain Hoy Stable, he was from the first crop of the recently imported Australian stallion, Royal Gem II, as was the race's favorite, Royal Bay Gem. This small black colt, owned by Texan Eugene Constantin Jr., may have turned in the Trial's best performance. He trailed more than fifteen lengths for four furlongs, got stuck in traffic, and was still seventh at the top of the stretch, yet fell short of third place by only a nose. C&G Stable's Money Broker upped his Derby stock, as well, having steadily improved his position from eighth to second.

Said Dark Star's trainer, Eddie Hayward, "I just wish they had run the Derby today."

Horsemen are a superstitious lot. Alfred Vanderbilt, for instance, didn't want anyone wishing him luck before a race. Mrs. Kercheval related a story that made for an ominous beginning to her husband's Derby week. He had unlocked the door to his room at the Brown Hotel and was surprised to see several reporters waiting inside. Mrs. Kercheval, who had remained at Sagamore to care for their children, told what happened next: "Ralph saw that someone had thrown a hat onto the bed and Ralph said, 'Oh, my God!' A hat on the bed is a red light to horsemen, you see." No doubt the reporters had great fun with it.

Native Dancer and Social Outcast weren't supposed to work out on Wednesday, the plan calling for a six-furlong gallop on Thursday. But two things changed Winfrey's mind: one, the weather forecast called for possible thunderstorms that day; and two, Native Dancer was threatening to demolish his stall.

So, following the third race on Wednesday, the stablemates walked onto the track to the delight of a surprised crowd. It was a walk-up start, beginning at the finish line on the mile oval. Winfrey ordered Bernie Everson to give Social Outcast a four-length head start, then drop The Dancer back to a six-length deficit on the backstretch before making a sustained drive in the stretch to pull even. While Everson sat still on the gray, Social Outcast posted lazy fractions of :26 2/5, :52, and 1:16 2/5 for six furlongs. At the top of the stretch, Everson gave The Dancer some slack. The colt closed in on his stablemate. A former jockey grounded by weight, Everson's instincts were to turn him loose and let him put Social Outcast away. But Winfrey wanted a sustained drive so The Dancer could feel the competition, and the two horses finished eye-to-eye in 1:39 3/5. Winfrey was pleased, but admitted he wished the first half had been quicker than the second.

Native Dancer's critics contended he was going all out at the end and couldn't get by Social Outcast. Nor did they think the time very remarkable. Maybe not, but his individual final quarter, clocked in :23 1/5, was.

Red Smith disagreed with the gloom and doom bunch. He predicted the work was a preview of the Derby. "After such a rehearsal," he said, "one could imagine the Derby itself being an anti-climax. As he leaned into the last turn and came romping to the wire, devouring the six-length lead he had conceded to his stablemate, he seemed to be running for the sheer joy of exercise." [3]

Anyway, it was too late for second guessing. The workout either put the colt on his toes or took the wind out of his sails.

A thunderstorm Thursday night left the track and barn area with soggy footing Friday morning, but a warming sun and Tom Young's crew had it dry in no time.

The numbers of reporters on the backside had swelled. This was the busiest day of the week, aside from Saturday. Several of the horses would be having their last serious works, and that afternoon, the Kentucky Oaks would be run (won by Calumet Farm's Bubbley, with Eddie Arcaro up). This also was the morning for shaping the Derby field. Beginning at 7 a.m., the official entries were to be dropped in the box in the racing secretary's office followed at 10 by the post-position draw.

The Dancer took his final gallop that morning, and later, Vanderbilt and Winfrey entertained the media. The horse was fine, Vanderbilt said, though he himself had a terrible cold. "If Native Dancer runs as fast as my nose is doing, we're in," he said.[4] Someone brought up the poor history of previously unbeaten juveniles, who either didn't make it to the Derby, lost it, or, in Morvich's case, won the roses but failed to win another race. In spite of the subject, Vanderbilt and Winfrey were so relaxed that it was well after 7 a.m. when someone reminded them of the deadline for entering the horses. Off they went to Lincoln Plaut's office.

Ace Destroyer was the first to be entered, and over the next two and a half hours, the field for the seventy-ninth Kentucky Derby became history. Next to be entered were the Irish-bred Curragh King, winner of the Arkansas Derby; the stretch-running Royal Bay Gem; Invigorator, for whom Bill Shoemaker was flying in from California to ride; Straight Face, with Teddy Atkinson aboard; and Ram o'War. Wally Dunn and Bill Winfrey dropped in the names of Correspondent, Native Dancer, and Social Outcast at about the same time. Jack Hodgins entered Spy Defense, but said he would scratch if the track was fast; ditto for Money Broker, said trainer Wright. Then there was a lull. As the clock crept toward 10, someone suggested looking for Eddie Hayward. Finally at 9:40, Hayward dropped in Dark Star's name, the final entry.

The post-position draw was televised live. Twelve

numbered pellets were drawn one at a time along with a horse's name. Correspondent drew post number two. Native Dancer was in stall seven with Money Broker next to him in eighth, followed to the outside by Social Outcast, Straight Face, Dark Star, and Royal Bay Gem. Dark Star's early speed might be compromised by his next-to-outside post.

Following the draw, the track's morning line odds showed the Vanderbilt entry at 3-5, Correspondent the second choice at 4-1, Royal Bay Gem, at 6-1, Dark Star, 8-1, and Straight Face and Money Broker at 15-1. Meteorologist O. K. Anderson still called for a possible off track for the Derby.

No problem. Native Dancer had run on a sloppy track before.

It all seemed so perfect.

CHAPTER 7

A Dark Star

Native Dancer's Derby day began at one in the morning with his usual four quarts of oats.

Les Murray watched him for a few minutes, talking to him as he always did. *I'll be back in a bit. Mister Bill got you down to gallop at 6:30.*

Thunderstorms during the night left standing puddles and a boggy track, but by 5 a.m., Murray could see a few stars. The air had been washed clean and from across the darkened race track, the lighted twin spires looked warm and friendly. Enough to give a man goose bumps.

Murray handed The Dancer a carrot, then sat on the floor next to a foreleg and began unwrapping the night bandages. Each time he removed a safety pin, he carefully pinned it to his left pants leg below the knee, lining them up in orderly rows. This made it easier to account for the pins. Such a small thing, a safety pin; but an open one on a stall floor can take a horse out of a race.

Winfrey arrived a short time later. He had Murray bring The Dancer out and walk him around. Winfrey ran a hand over him, then watched him walk some more. Native Dancer moved freely, and if the big gray colt had tied up the day before, he showed no sign of it during his Derby morning jog. [1]

When it was light enough, Tom Young's crew was out wringing the water from the track. The new forecast was promising: clearing skies and a breeze from the southwest would have the surface in good shape by the day's first race at 11:30.

From the top of the stretch came the sounds of metal slamming against metal and clanging bells. Starter R. W. (Ruby) White and his crew had begun checking the starting gates. With the Derby on national television, White wasn't about to make any mistakes.

Technicians also were out early setting up equipment for CBS' coverage, which was set to begin at 4 p.m. The network's local affiliate, WHAS-TV, would be on the air earlier with the day's undercard. The bulky cameras were set up at several locations, including the grandstand's roof. Unfortunately there was no video taping then. And while some tracks had installed stewards' films, Churchill Downs wouldn't have them until the next year. Among the gaps in the coverage was the clubhouse turn.

By 6 a.m., the news media converged upon the barn area in huge numbers. About two hours later, each Derby horse's identification number, tattooed inside the upper lip, was checked. The Dancer's: F6888.

Not everyone was delighted to see the sun and hear the new forecast call for a fast track by the Derby's 4:30 post time. Spy Defense was scratched, the only defection; trainer Vester (Tennessee) Wright decided to give Money Broker a chance. So did Bill Winfrey with Social Outcast. Young's crew did such a good job that the track was listed as "fast" by the first race.

Around mid-afternoon, Bill Winfrey accompanied his wife and two friends to the grandstand so they might find their seats in ample time. They followed the same route the horses would be taking on the "walk over" to the paddock, walking next to the outer rail around the first and second turns. The fifth race was

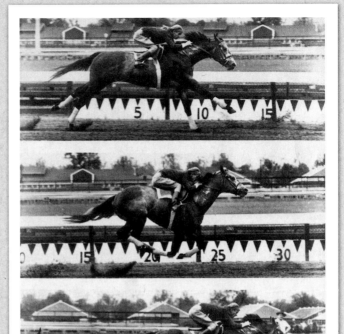

Native Dancer, known to his fans as "The Gray Ghost," had his stride measured by a *LIFE* magazine photographer (above). His stride of twenty-nine feet bested even Man o' War's stride.

Native Dancer descends in tail male from foundation sire Phalaris through his grandsire Unbreakable (top) and sire Polynesian (above). Discovery (above right), the broodmare sire of Native Dancer, was a top handicap horse for Sagamore Farm. Geisha (right, with a 1953 full sister to Native Dancer) passed on her gray coloring to her distinguished son.

Alfred Vanderbilt's Sagamore Farm, as it appeared in the 1950s (below), with the quarter-mile indoor training track in the center. And the same building in 1998 (above and right) still painted in Vanderbilt's colors.

Alfred Vanderbilt (far left) hired young trainer Bill Winfrey (left) in 1949. Just three years later, Native Dancer arrived in Winfrey's barn. Winfrey later trained for the Wheatley and Phipps stables, replacing the legendary trainer Sunny Jim Fitzsimmons (above).

Eric Guerin (right) rode Native Dancer in all but one of the colt's starts. Eddie Arcaro (below right) worked The Dancer prior to the American Derby, his only race aboard the colt.
Arcaro and Guerin are highlighted in the 1953 Kentucky Derby jockeys group photo (bottom).
Native Dancer (below) wore a protective "hat" when travelling.

Native Dancer captured the Youthful Stakes (opposite, top) at Jamaica in only his second start, then stormed through the Saratoga juvenile stakes, taking the Flash (opposite, middle), Saratoga Special (above), and Grand Union Hotel (below) in a two and a half-week span.

The Dancer concluded his Saratoga campaign with a Hopeful victory (below), then moved his attack to Belmont Park where he captured the Anticipation Purse (bottom) and Futurity. He closed out his two-year-old season with a win in the East View Stakes (left) at Jamaica and earned co-Horse of the Year honors.

Native Dancer went into the Kentucky Derby as the odds-on favorite after a decisive victory in the Wood Memorial (above), but a troubled trip and a horse named Dark Star conspired to give the gray colt his only career loss (top). Native Dancer rebounded with an easy Withers score (below) as he prepared for the Preakness.

The Preakness was another hard-fought race for The Dancer (below), but this time, he returned victorious (left). His connections, including Guerin, Vanderbilt, and Winfrey (from center to far right), celebrated in the winner's circle.

On a wet, dreary New York day, Native Dancer showed his grit in the Belmont Stakes (below left) and returned once again to the winner's circle for Vanderbilt (below right). Then it was on to the Dwyer (above) for yet another triumph.

Native Dancer romped by nine lengths in the Arlington Classic (below), then virtually repeated the performance at Saratoga in the Travers (above).

As a four-year-old, Native Dancer added the Metropolitan (above) to his list of impressive victories. As the stable star, The Dancer received plenty of attention (below), especially from his groom Les Murray (right, kneeling) and exercise rider Bernie Everson (right, standing).

Native Dancer's influence as a sire extends not only through his sons, such as Raise a Native (below), but also through his daughters, such as Natalma (above), dam of the immortal Northern Dancer. Europe's great racehorse Sea-Bird (left), a grandson of Native Dancer, helped establish the sire line there.

Native Dancer may have lost the Derby, but later generations have more than made up for it. Among his Derby-winning descendants are (clockwise from top right) Real Quiet, Alysheba, Fusaichi Pegasus, and Thunder Gulch.

The Gray Ghost in his paddock at Sagamore Farm in Maryland. He is buried on the property.

NATIVE DANCER

1950 ⟷ 1967

just ending, and Winfrey motioned that they should go under the fence to avoid the horses pulling up on the turn. Here they met some boys, likely the sons of grooms and exercise riders, sitting in the grass. "Want a tip on the Derby, lady?" one of the boys asked Elaine Winfrey. "Dark Star. Native Dancer's not gonna win it."

"You shouldn't say things like that," Elaine Winfrey scolded.

"They don't know what they're talking about." Bill said, taking her arm.[2]

In front of the clubhouse, they met Dark Star's owner, Captain Harry Guggenheim. He was headed to the stables and told Bill he would wait for him so they could walk back together.

"He's the nicest man," Winfrey commented a few minutes later.

The official estimate placed the capacity-plus crowd at 105,000, which held the Vanderbilt duo around 3-5. Correspondent's odds, in the meantime, dropped from 4-1 to 7-2 following an impressive workout on Friday of five furlongs in 1:00 3/5. Royal Bay Gem's odds also dropped from 6-1 to 7-2; but the biggest surprise had to be the lack of support for Dark Star. Eight-to-one following his win in the Trial, he would close at 25-1.

Around 3 p.m., Les Murray stood on an overturned bucket and began braiding The Dancer's mane. Native Dancer didn't give his affections freely, and Les Murray felt utterly privileged. They had formed a bond that only horse people could fully comprehend. Visitors cringed whenever they saw Murray pulling his 200-pound frame up using The Dancer's tail. Murray would just smile and say, "We knows each other lak a book."

A little after 3:30 the horses for the seventh race began the "walk over." Harold Walker and Les Murray led the big gray out of his stall. Another groom brought out Social Outcast, the gelded chestnut son of Shut Out and Pansy.

Turf writers David Woods, Red Smith, and Frank Graham had been spending much of the afternoon at Barn 16. Now with the gray headed for the paddock, they decided to take a shortcut across the infield. "As we ducked under the rail," Woods wrote later, "a youngster called to Winfrey: 'Hey mister! Dark Star's gonna beat you.' We all heard the remark but paid no attention; that is, no one except Red, who made it the theme of his column the next day..." [3]

According to Joe Hirsch, it's about a mile from the barn area to the paddock and "takes anywhere from twenty minutes to a half-hour. The old saddling paddock [in the early 1950s] was terrible. It was open on the sides; the rear of the stalls weren't closed and the public could easily access the horses if not for the guards. There was very little space in the walking ring outside the stalls."

Royal Bay Gem was the first to go over. The little black colt was a local favorite. His sire, Royal Gem II, had been a top stayer in Australia and was imported in 1949 to stand at Warner L. Jones' Hermitage Farm near Goshen, about fifteen miles north of Louisville. His rider, twenty-six year-old Jim Combest, was Louisville-born. The colt's closing style seemed tailor-made for the 1,320-foot long stretch, and he would go off the third choice at 6.80-1. Native Dancer, the fifth to arrive, received a rousing ovation.

The last horse to reach the paddock, as he had been the last horse entered, was Dark Star. Bred by Warner Jones, the son of Royal Gem II wouldn't be in the Derby field had it not been for Dr. Alex Harthill's prompt action. His dam, Isolde, was unable to deliver, and Harthill cut the foal out of her, saving both lives.

Harry Guggenheim came to own him by mistake. It seems there were two similar looking brown colts among the yearlings being sold by Warner Jones. Guggenheim purchased one of them, but his van later picked up the wrong horse. When Jones discovered the error he offered to make the switch, but Guggenheim liked this one and decided to keep him. It was Dark Star.

During the last-minute instructions, Winfrey reminded Eric Guerin that The Dancer had the versatility to take the lead if anybody tried to get away with soft fractions. It was this multifaceted talent that led one Turf scribe, Walter Stewart of the *Memphis Commercial Appeal,* to write, "Native Dancer could stop at the quarter-poles and put on the hula-hula for the crowd and still win going away." As for Social Outcast, Johnny Adams was to go on with him, and maybe the mates would finish one-two.

Guerin was a Cajun boy, born in 1924 in Maringuoin, Louisiana, a little town between Baton Rouge and Opelousas. He'd left home at fourteen to be a jockey and by 1946 had topped the jockey standings for stakes winners. The next year he won the Derby aboard Jet Pilot, then finished unplaced with On The Mark in 1950. Now twenty-nine, he still had the shy smile and freckle-faced freshness that fit his laid-back personality. At five feet, four inches, he was taller than most jockeys and battled weight most of his career. His was never the household name of an Eddie Arcaro or Bill Shoemaker, but any trainer would tell you he was as good as any of them, especially his coolness under pressure.

The call came for "riders up." The fans yelled and clapped and shouted "Go Dancer!" and flashbulbs popped. The gray tossed his head, as if to tell them to save it for the winner's circle.

Promptly at 4:20 p.m., "Boots and Saddles" called the field to the track. The Dancer led the field through the tunnel, with Harold Walker on one shank and Murray the other. An outrider took The Dancer's lead, and the combined bands from Fort Knox, University of Louisville, and Flaget High School struck up "My Old Kentucky Home." Murray and Walker gave the gray parting pats; Murray whispered, *C'mon you big bum. Don't disappoint all these folks who come to see you win.* Both men hunkered down next to the fence near the clubhouse turn where the other grooms would join them. "He's gonna win for sure," Murray vowed, "...if nothing happens."

Ace Destroyer, with Job Dean Jessop in the irons, followed Native Dancer, then came Correspondent with a confident Arcaro up. The heavily campaigned Ram o'War had Doug Dodson aboard, and Invigorator had the services of Bill Shoemaker. Next was the Irish-bred Curragh King, with Dave Erb up, the longest shot on the board at 99-1. The Florida Derby winner, Money Broker, seemed overlooked at 45.80-1. Al Popara, his rider, had learned only yesterday that he had been suspended ten days by the Churchill Downs stewards for rough riding in Thursday's seventh race. He was glad it didn't begin until Monday.

Straight Face, with Teddy Atkinson up, followed, then Dark Star with Henry Moreno aboard. This was Moreno's first Derby ride, and the Chicago-born son of an Italian barber had instructions from trainer Eddie Hayward to settle the colt just off the pace. He glanced toward the stands and wished his wife were there. Unable to get a baby sitter for their two-year-old son, Michael, she would be watching on television from the tourist camp out on U.S. Highway 42, their home for the past week. Royal Bay Gem brought up the back of the parade. No one doubted his ability to go ten furlongs, if only jockey Jim Combest could keep him from losing sight of the field.

"Grab that paper!" Ruby White yelled to one of his assistants. A gust of wind had blown the sheet at the starting gate and a crewman nabbed it. "This headwind...will cut down the time of this Derby," one of the assistants said to Tommy Fitzgerald of the *Louisville Courier-Journal*. The breeze had picked up, and White made the decision to "lower the locks." It was a procedure that made it easier for the doors to open, but also made it easier for a horse to break through. "...we have a crewman for every horse to keep him in his stall," White said. He tested the doors again. Perfect.

The start for the Kentucky Derby comes from a gate set up at the top of the stretch. At 120 feet, it is the widest section of the entire track, able to accommodate two gates, each holding fourteen horses. Just one gate was needed today. As the horses limbered up on the far turn, White handed each crewman instructions according to the horse he would be handling. He studied his own marked-up sheet listing each starter's gate behavior history. The horses ended their gallop and fell into line once more as they approached the gate. White mounted the green starter's platform.

"It is now post time," a voice crackled over the loudspeakers. The crowd roared. White checked his watch: 4:32 p.m. Two minutes late.

Ace Destroyer quietly loaded into his number one stall, followed in rapid succession by Correspondent and Ram o'War. Just as Invigorator went in, Ram o'War broke through, but an assistant starter hung onto him. The colt was reloaded so quickly the whole process barely missed a beat. With Spy Defense's scratch, Native Dancer now loaded into stall six. Only four winners had come from six; none since Flying Ebony in 1925.

Guerin pulled down his goggles and readied for that split second when the doors open and the bottom seems to drop out from under you, as half a ton of power suddenly explodes out of the gate. Ahead lay a quarter mile of empty track. Quiet now, but in about a minute and a half, it would be a tunnel of noise.

White picked up an extension cord with a button

attached to batteries and connected to the starting gate mechanism. Hardly had Royal Bay Gem gone in when White pushed the button. He checked his watch. It was 4:32.30.

CHAPTER 8

"...although probably best."

I t was the quickest start ever for a field this size: thirty seconds for the eleven horses, Ram o'War's breaking through included, and, except for Ace Destroyer slightly bumping Correspondent, a perfect one.

The plans were for Dark Star to run in third early on, and Guerin was to have Native Dancer well-placed just off the leaders going into the first turn. Instead, Dark Star flew to the front, angled over to the rail, and so dictated the race from there on. Native Dancer actually broke the quickest, but lost all speed and advantage. When Winfrey looked for him as the field raced past the grandstand, he found him hemmed in back in sixth. Winfrey shook his head.

Someone once said the first turn is no place for 'nervous Nellies;' where every jockey in the race wants the same piece of ground every other jockey either has or wants. Dark Star led Correspondent into the turn by more than a length, both free of traffic. But Native Dancer, still sixth, split the fifth- and seventh-placed horses, Money Broker slightly to the front on his outside and Curragh King on the rail. The latter bore out, taking The Dancer with him. At that moment, Money Broker came in sharply and collided with the gray.

"There were a lot of horses together when we hit the turn," Al Popara recalled, "and I couldn't get back of Guerin's horse. So I tried to circle him. I actually thought we had cleared Native Dancer all right, but my horse changed stride and I heard Guerin yell 'Hey' when he checked his horse...It seemed like he was on the inside of me one second and on the outside the next." [1]

Trainer Tennessee Wright wanted Popara to keep Money Broker on "the inside rail to save ground on the clubhouse turn...This was the strategy we used in winning the Florida Derby. I was trying to take back far enough to drop in over The 'Dancer's' heels where I could save ground but my horse was to [sic] rank.

"Funny. Native Dancer had previously showed more speed, so I didn't expect him to be that far back of the leaders."

Guerin had to take up on The Dancer, and in the process, he lost two positions in the run to the second corner. As Dark Star reached the top of the backstretch, with six furlongs remaining, eleven lengths separated him from Native Dancer. Guerin reined his colt to the outside and asked him to run. Native Dancer responded with a :23 flat move over the third quarter, a run that took him from eighth to fourth. Winfrey later said that he "ran like a wild horse."

Dark Star had peeled off the opening quarters in :23 4/5 and :24. Henry Moreno successfully slowed him down to :25 flat for the third and maintained his length and a half lead over Correspondent. Native Dancer made another move on the outside and went by Straight Face as the field swept into the far turn. Then Guerin sought to save ground and again dropped The Dancer in on the rail. Dark Star hit the mile in 1:36 3/5. Here, Arcaro asked Correspondent to run, but the colt came up empty, and as he struggled to save his position, Native Dancer came up on his inside and into second place.

Rookies hear veterans talk about the "tunnel of noise," that final quarter-mile run down the home-stretch through a volume of noise from more than

100,000 voices, and into the tunnel the "rookie" Moreno and Dark Star went. Dark Star's stride was beginning to chop a little, and he drifted out from the rail about fifteen feet. Moreno looked under his right arm; Correspondent was no threat. But where was the gray horse? He looked to his left.

Guerin was gunning Native Dancer toward the hole with nothing between them and the finish line but empty track. Moreno knew one thing: If he gets in there, it's all over. He steered Dark Star to the inside. The eighth pole flashed by — maybe twelve, thirteen seconds left to run.

With the opening gone, Guerin took Native Dancer to the outside, yet again losing momentum and ground. At the furlong pole, Guerin called on the colt to fire. He was shocked when he didn't get an answer. At the sixteenth-pole Guerin gave him two, three good whacks. This time, he got a response.

Railbirds always swore they could see the bottoms of Native Dancer's front feet when he was really going. And in the final sixteenth of the Kentucky Derby, the railbirds could see the bottoms of his front feet. Native Dancer was running faster than he ever had before.

Well back in sixth and trying to keep Money Broker from retreating any farther, Al Popara could see some of the action ahead. "I was at the eighth pole…and I saw the gray chasing after the leader and [heard] the roar of the crowd. There always is the roar on Derby Day, but this was a ROAR!"

Moreno heard the roar, too. He glanced back and saw the gray closing rapidly. He knew Dark Star was giving everything he had, but he popped him once with the whip, then buried his face in the wonderful colt's dark flowing mane. Vanderbilt, Kercheval, the Winfreys all watched helplessly as Native Dancer reeled the colt in with every stride, saw him pull alongside, saw him thrust his head forward just as they hit the finish line.

"Did he get there?" Vanderbilt asked.

"We got beat," Winfrey replied soberly.

"Photo" flashed on the tote board, with the numbers 10 and 1 blinking, in that order. It seemed an eternity, and yet all too soon all the numbers stopped blinking — 10, 1, and 5. Invigorator getting up for third, five lengths back.

Dark Star's 2:02 clocking was only three ticks off Whirlaway's track record, the fifth fastest in seventy-nine renewals, and still a time that holds up very well.

The likes of Seattle Slew, Spectacular Bid, Swale, Ferdinand, Alysheba, and Winning Colors all have run slower. Dark Star ran the final quarter in :25 2/5. By all eyewitness accounts, Native Dancer covered the final half-furlong in a record pace.

Churchill Downs was unearthly quiet until both gladiators returned from their epic struggle; Native Dancer to the scales for unsaddling, Dark Star to the winner's circle. The few fans who had wagered on Dark Star were rewarded handsomely, $51.80, the fourth highest payout until then.

Reality sunk in, then shock when Dark Star stood in front of the pagoda, draped in roses. The Derby winner's circle, the most hallowed in racing. A piece of ground used only once a year by a horse that gets only one shot at it. It is this very fine line, one split second in the race, that adds to the Derby's mystique.

The repercussions weren't long in coming. Popara knew it when he was at the sixteenth-pole and heard that unbelievable roar. He had one thought in mind: "I sure hope he [Native Dancer] wins it because if he gets beat something unseemly is going to hit the fan. He didn't and it did."

Native Dancer had just begun the walk to the barn when he stopped and looked back.

Skeptics say it was a noise or something that distracted him. But Les Murray always insisted The Dancer was looking at the winner's circle and was visibly upset long after the race. Guerin noticed a change as well. "It's really strange," he said, "until that day he was the laziest horse in a workout you could find — always playing, never serious. But there was no more foolishness after the Derby. From that moment on, whatever you asked him to do in a workout he did." [2]

It was a long walk from their box to the unsaddling area, longer still as Vanderbilt and Winfrey mustered smiles for the hundreds offering sympathies. In the tunnel, they met up with Ed Hayward and Captain Guggenheim. Vanderbilt extended his hand. "If it had to be anybody, Harry, I'm glad it was you."

After weighing out, Guerin searched for his bosses. Winfrey sure wanted to talk with him, too, but his first concern was with the horses, and he went straight to the barn. Fighting back tears, Guerin told Vanderbilt what happened, at least the way he saw it, which was as an intentional act by Money Broker's jockey.

Popara saw them talking as he made his way to the dressing room. "I still remember Vanderbilt looking over Guerin's shoulder at me and if looks could kill I never would have made it." Popara wished that Churchill Downs had the stewards' film patrol — they began in 1954 — for the film clear him of foul claims. But the only film available then was newsreel and CBS' footage; neither of which had a camera placed where the incident could be seen with any clarity.

In the showers, Popara explained to Guerin how his horse "changed strides on me as I passed him and he told me he didn't believe it."

Henry Moreno said it was Dark Star who decided how he wanted to run the race, but admitted to being "plenty scared" at the sixteenth pole. He wasn't sure he had won until he went under the wire, "but I knew it then and wasn't worried about the photo."

The rest, in the order they finished: Shoemaker said Invigorator was "bottled up once;" Jimmy Combest said he let Royal Bay Gem drop too far back; Arcaro couldn't explain Correspondent's lack of run; Ted Atkinson offered no excuses for sixth-place Straight Face, but the gelding was later favoring his chronic knee; Social Outcast lacked any speed; Money Broker was used up early; then came Ram o'War, Curragh King, and Ace Destroyer.

No one ever denied that Dark Star ran a super race, but few believed then, and to this day, that the best horse won. Even Don Fair's *Daily Racing Form* trip notes indicated that Native Dancer was "probably best." [3]

Walter Haight of the *Louisville Courier-Journal* thought The Dancer had "the roughest trip of an odds-on favorite since Bimelech went to his knees at the start and became a victim of Gallahadion." While Dark Star's race and time were remarkable, Native Dancer, "given clear sailing, not only might have won, but chances are he would have set a new mark in the bargain." As for the clubhouse turn incident, Haight thought it was relevant only in the events it triggered.

Those events pointed increasingly to Eric Guerin's ride. One Churchill Downs board member was overheard after the race saying, "He took that colt everywhere on the track except the ladies' room."

Courier-Journal reporter Al Coffman echoed those sentiments, writing that Guerin "was all over the track with The Dancer. First he was on the outside, then the inside. Finally, when he saw that Moreno might cut him off by drifting to the rail, Guerin went back to the outside and there The Dancer made his final gallant bid."

Turf writer George Ryall agreed with Walter Haight that the incident "started a sequence of mishaps the grey never overcame." While Ryall defended Guerin as a rider, he thought he handled The Dancer "badly" in the Derby and that the bumping unsettled the jockey more than it did Native Dancer. "Apparently it knocked Guerin's plan of campaign right out of his head, for he did something I wouldn't have believed unless I saw it; and then it was hardly credible.

"In the backstretch he made three separate runs with Native Dancer — in one of them, at the half-mile ground, he ran into a pocket — and in the stretch he made another! You can't do things like that, and bring them off successfully, even with an extraordinary horse."

Vanderbilt first believed the incident was premeditated, but later disagreed with some who thought the race was lost then. He told Arthur Daley of *The New York Times* that when the field turned the far corner, Eric "lost confidence in the horse and began cutting corners." Instead of taking the outside route that had won him eleven straight races, Guerin went inside. "He should have said to himself, 'This isn't an ordinary horse. This is the Dancer. He can still win from the outside.' " [4]

Winfrey "never blamed Eric," his son Carey said. "He managed to act like these things just happen, though it must have killed him inside." Carey, only eleven in 1953, learned from the Derby that "life throws some pretty nasty curve balls, but...if you take them with dignity, as my father certainly did, you can go on...and overcome."

Dr. Alex Harthill, who has treated dozens of Derby horses, said Guerin, "didn't have a damn thing to do with it [the loss]." Forty years later he was still convinced Native Dancer lost because he "tied up badly" the day before.

Some questioned whether the colt himself was fit. The late Jim Bolus, the Derby's great historian, believed that with The Dancer's ankles being fired, Winfrey had to play catch up, and, "seemingly desperate, was working this big, powerful colt frequently during this time — maybe too frequently."

This writer talked with Winfrey in October of 1989 and brought up the inevitable. His answer came as a surprise. "I didn't have him fit," he said simply. Joe Hirsch, however, doubts that the horse was unfit to race. "Bill Winfrey was a brilliant horseman [and] as for Alfred Vanderbilt...[he] would not have allowed Native Dancer to run in the Derby if he wasn't fit."

It was more likely a long chain of circumstances beginning with the ankles being fired and culminating in the events that arose from the bumping. The fact that he so very nearly overcame it all speaks volumes for the kind of racehorse Native Dancer was.

Later that long, awful day, Eric Guerin stopped by Native Dancer's stall. He reached in his pocket and handed him a carrot. "I'm sorry we got beat. You were the best, champ."

CHAPTER 9

Redemption

T he rains that had been predicted for the Derby arrived the next day. It was still drizzling at noon on Monday, May 4, when Native Dancer boarded a rail car at the same siding where he had arrived a week earlier. Even the weather seemed to have been written for the occasion: gray, wet, gloomy. No hero's sendoff, just a couple of photographers and several staunch fans cheering their fallen paladin on to redemption at Pimlico. Traveling with him were Social Outcast, Winfrey's lead pony and fox terrier, and Invigorator. Straight Face was making the trip, too, his bandaged ailing knee better now.

Nor was there appropriate fanfare for the Derby winner, at either of his sendoffs. As the cars carrying the Dark Star and some other horses were coupled to the New York-bound train at Louisville's Union Station, one of the two-year-olds loaded with Dark Star became so frightened by the noise that the car had to return to the siding to be unloaded. The Derby winner departed again later that afternoon.

With three weeks separating the Derby and the Preakness, the schedules for the Pimlico-bound horses varied. Ed Hayward's immediate plan called for Dark Star to run in the Preakness Prep on May 18, along with Royal Bay Gem and Ram o'War. Tennessee Wright said Money Broker would probably race at Churchill Downs a couple of times before the meeting ended on May 16. Money Broker and the gray never crossed paths again.

As for the gray, Bill Winfrey planned to work on Native Dancer's speed over the next couple of weeks, then prep for the Preakness using the mile Withers Stakes at Belmont on May 16.

Before returning to New York the day after the Derby, Vanderbilt is said to have promised Churchill officials he would be back with Derby-winning sons of Native Dancer. He was only partly right. Sons and grandsons, even a great-grandaughter, have avenged the loss, but none belonged to him. Alfred Vanderbilt never had another Derby entry.

Vanderbilt did go to Jamaica on Monday, where it must have been as difficult running a gauntlet of well-meaning sympathizers as it had been after the Derby. *Thoroughbred Record* journalist Bob Horwood thought Vanderbilt handled it with grace, even when Vanderbilt agreed to talk with him.

Horwood was something of a thorn in Vanderbilt's side when it came to Native Dancer. He contended the gray had yet a great deal to prove, which Vanderbilt insisted during the interview that the colt would do by year's end. "...but right now, he didn't win the Derby, so you are right. And that's that."

Horwood disagreed. "He certainly ran a much better race than I believed he was fit to run. In fact, he ran a winning race, though he didn't win." Before their conversation ended, Vanderbilt convinced him that the colt was sound.[1]

The next day, Horwood found Eric Guerin in the jockeys' dressing room and wanted his point of view. Patiently, Eric replayed the race, the 'incident,' but concluded the trouble was with The Dancer himself. "He just wasn't himself. He wouldn't give me anything coming out of the gate...Then, in the backstretch, he reached for the bit and started to move some." The conversation had attracted several other jocks in the room, and Guerin turned to Atkinson (who rode Straight Face). "Remember when you looked back, coming to the three and a half? I was still on the outside then and scuffling, but he wouldn't give."

Atkinson nodded. "But the next thing I saw, you were going by Eddie and me on the inside as though we were tied to the fence." Guerin insisted he had to go to the inside, after which Native Dancer "spit out the bit…Then he got to running like himself in the last sixteenth." When Horwood implied Native Dancer might have been hurting, Guerin didn't believe he could have leveled off as he did a couple of times with such speed if he was hurting. "And," he added, "he cooled out wonderful." [2]

With the Preakness still nearly three weeks away, the field continued to shape up.

On Saturday, May 9, Royal Bay Gem came from far back to win the Jersey Stakes by two lengths in the mud. On the following Monday, Tahitian King beat Isasmoothie in the Swift Stakes.

A few days earlier, on May 6, Jamie K. won his first

race of the year after seven attempts. Bob Horwood liked Jamie K. and predicted the colt would improve with distance, if the rangy bay learned to behave in the gate. Jamie K. had acted up before the Wood Memorial, then had been rank with jockey Conn McCreary at the start, and finished next to last. So, trainer John Partridge went to the one rider well-known for his ability to handle problem horses. When Jamie K. broke his drought winning the May 6 mile and one-sixteenth allowance, Eddie Arcaro was on board.

It couldn't have come at a more opportune time for Arcaro, having just recently been "fired" by Wally Dunn, who was dissatisfied with the jockey's ride on Correspondent in the Derby. With Jamie K. scheduled for another allowance at Belmont Park on May 13, Partridge pegged him for the ride. Arcaro suggested taking the blinkers off the colt, and the duo won impressively by three and a half lengths.

The starting gate for a mile race at Belmont Park is set up on the backstretch. That was why television viewers had a better view of the only drama contained in the Withers Stakes on May 16.

Only three started, Native Dancer, Invigorator, and

Real Brother, making it the shortest Withers field since Count Fleet whipped two others in 1943. With win betting only, the crowd of 38,044 sent the gray off at 1-20. The race was little more than a workout for The Dancer, the only scare coming when he stumbled leaving the gate. Winfrey had been sharpening his early speed over the last two weeks, and the colt was just a little overanxious. He recovered quickly and likely would have taken the lead then had Guerin not taken back on him. Still full of run, the gray "went to the front from his position on the outside when ready and briskly drew clear to win with authority..." [3] He won by four over Invigorator in 1:36 1/5 and though he walked back perfectly, Bill Winfrey was seen checking the colt's ankles in the winner's circle.

George Ryall, writing in *The Blood-Horse*, was impressed and thought the colt looked better and "higher in flesh than he did three or four weeks ago."

The Gray Ghost was back.

In the Preakness Prep on Monday, May 18, Royal Bay Gem beat Dark Star by three-quarters of a length in 1:46 1/5, more than four seconds slower than the track mark.

On Wednesday, May 20, the day after arriving at

Pimlico, Native Dancer galloped before a large and admiring crowd. One of those most impressed was Clyde Troutt, trainer of Royal Bay Gem. "Look at that big horse," he told George Bowen of the *Louisville Courier-Journal*. "There ought to be a law making such a horse give weight to my little one." Then, on a serious note, he added, "It was a shame for a horse like that to be beaten. It was just one of those unlucky breaks." He also thought The Dancer had appeared a little drawn at Louisville.

The next morning, the gray went out in the fog to work six furlongs and drew an even larger audience, from *Daily Racing Form* clockers to stable hands. Although The Dancer had stretched out to his full immense stride, there was still the impression of untapped resources. Two different times were taken, Winfrey's of 1:11 4/5, and the *Form*'s 1:11 3/5, both just off the track record of 1:10 1/5.

Troutt was overheard saying, "He didn't have to do that — just looking at him is enough to scare me." The consensus was that The Dancer looked better than he had at Louisville, even a little arrogant, and as he walked back to the barn, awfully damn sure of himself.

On Pimlico's opening day on October 25, 1870, a

colt named Preakness won the Dinner Party Stakes, the first stakes race offered at the new track. Three years later, on May 27, Survivor beat six opponents in the inaugural running of the race named for Preakness by ten lengths, still the biggest margin in the race's history. Except for the years 1891 through 1893, the Preakness has been run ever since.

Eighty years after that first Preakness, Native Dancer and six opponents were loaded into the gate for the seventy-seventh renewal. Although an overnight rain left the track deep in mud, it was officially listed as fast by post time. One veteran observer, however, said it was as "dead as a cracked golf ball."

The seven entries loaded quickly from the rail out, starting with Royal Bay Gem, the second favorite at 11.20-1; Jamie K., with Arcaro up, fourth choice at 16.60; Dark Star, a surprising 11.30; Native Dancer in the fourth stall, 1-5; Ram o'War, the longest shot in the field; Correspondent, with Bob Summers up; and Tahitian King.

As expected, Royal Bay Gem brought up the rear, some sixteen lengths off the pace, with Jamie K. keeping him company. Dark Star was comfortable on the lead again, so Moreno let him go. Tahitian King ran in the second spot and Guerin tucked Native Dancer into third, with Correspondent lapped on him. When Tahitian King drifted away from the rail going around the far turn, Guerin moved The Dancer toward the opening. Although jockey Headley Woodhouse made a quick move to close it again, it was too late. The Dancer moved into second at the top of the stretch.

Dark Star still had the lead, but it suddenly began to evaporate, then disappeared altogether. Native Dancer found himself in front with nothing to run at. His ears bounced forward. Guerin cocked the whip and shouted to him. Now he could hear the crowd noise rise several decibels and glanced back to see Jamie K. coming like an express train. After a couple of good whacks, the gray returned to business.

The chart shows that Native Dancer had a head lead in mid-stretch and stretched it to a long neck at the wire. The final time, 1:57 4/5, was nearly two seconds off Capot's track standard, but The Dancer ran the final furlong at a :12 4/5 clip. Royal Bay Gem got up to be third, six lengths behind Jamie K. Ram o'War surprised for fourth, and Dark Star was fifth, nearly ten lengths behind the winner. Correspondent, his best race obviously left behind in the Blue Grass at Keeneland, trailed Tahitian King by eight lengths.

Guerin said afterward that Dark Star's sudden stop put Native Dancer in the lead sooner than he wanted. Vanderbilt was still a bit shaky, though. "I didn't think Jamie K. would get that close...He's better than I thought he was. I'm really proud of my horse, trainer, my jock, groom, farm and everything else." [4]

Talking with Turf writer Red Smith over the telephone, Bill Winfrey admitted that the race was "a little tight...and Jamie K. surprised me — raw-ther!" Later, he admitted being more impressed with The Dancer's effort in the Derby. [5]

Unfortunately Dark Star bowed a tendon at the top of the stretch and was retired to stud, which led some of The Dancer's critics to contend that Dark Star would have beaten him again. But the circumstances were different. The gray had a good trip in the Preakness and was already making his move on the leader when Dark Star sustained his injury.

The rest would get their chance in the Belmont Stakes. Longer race, longer stretch.

CHAPTER 10

The Test Of Champions

Colonel Richard Nicolls seemed hardly the type to be pegged as the "Father of the American Turf." He was a military man, the first English governor of New York. Yet less than a year after Peter Stuyvesant surrendered the Dutch colony, New Amsterdam, on September 8, 1664, Nicolls had laid out the first formal racecourse in the colonies. He called it New Market after the track in his homeland and established it on Hempstead Plain, described in 1665 as being "sixteen miles long and four broad...toward the middle of Long Island." [1]

At first, races were held once a year, but Nicolls soon announced that the winners of the top races, to be run each spring and fall, would be awarded a silver cup, to encourage "the bettering of the breed of horses, which through great neglect has been impaired."

One has to wonder what Nicolls would have

thought about Belmont Park when it opened on May 4, 1905, on 650 acres in Hempstead Township. Could he have imagined such a facility? A mile and a half track, the largest in the country; a 650-foot grandstand; a clubhouse with dining rooms, bedrooms, and balconies; turf and field clubs; a separate one-mile training track; and a seven-furlong straight course.[2]

A crowd of 40,000 attended Belmont's opening day, headlined by immortal Sysonby dueling Race King to a dead heat in the Metropolitan Handicap, which had been moved from old Morris Park. Twenty days later, the thirty-ninth Belmont Stakes, which also had been run at Morris, debuted at the track bearing its name and produced the last filly to win, Tanya.

The mile and a half main track is still the largest in the country, and the Belmont Stakes has become one of the most important races on a three-year-old's schedule. Everyone may want to win the Derby, but it's the Belmont that is known as "The Test of Champions." Its twelve furlongs are what many breeders want to see in the bloodlines. For Native Dancer, it was an opportunity to silence those who still questioned his stamina and his class.

Winfrey brought him up to the race in the three weeks following the Preakness with a regimen of walks, gallops, and sprints. A mile on June 1 in 1:44 1/5 with an added furlong in 1:57 3/5; a ten-furlong work four days later; and on June 9, the Belmont distance in 2:38 2/5. In his last timed prep on the day before the June 13 race, he went six furlongs in 1:13 2/5.

Ram o'War, Jamie K., and Royal Bay Gem, an impressive recent winner of the Peabody Memorial Stakes, were back from Pimlico. The new faces were The Preem, owned by bandleader Louis Prima and the longest shot on the board at 122.45-1, and the black Polynesian colt from King Ranch, Kamehameha, whose name race callers generally shortened to "the K horse."

Belmont Park was The Dancer's home base throughout his career, specifically Barn 20, stall number six, equipped with electric fans to see him through the summers and screens to keep out the flies. The fans weren't needed on Belmont day, however. George Ryall wrote in *The Blood-Horse* that it "was as thoroughly disagreeable a day for an important race as I've suffered through…" It was still raining when the horses were being saddled.

Often likened to a battleship, Native Dancer never looked more like one than he did in the hard gray downpour of the Belmont Stakes post parade. On his toes more than usual, he fairly rippled with power. Still, that unknown factor remained, and he was sent off at only 9-20, with Jamie K. less than 3-1.

Royal Bay Gem and Native Dancer broke the quickest from the starting gate set up at the finish line. Ram o'War led the "K" horse in the 833-foot run to the first corner by a couple of lengths. But the Polynesian colt's saddle started slipping, and he began retreating to last place. The big surprise was Jamie K. While Ram o'War sleepwalked through fractions of :25, :50 1/5, and 1:15, Jamie K. was running in third after being hustled away from the gate with Arcaro casting furtive backward glances to see where The Dancer was. His intentions were clear, but Guerin, just a couple of lengths back, wasn't going to fall for it.

Ram o'War was finished after the mile in 1:39 2/5. Jamie K. slipped into the lead, Native Dancer into second. Sensing another dog fight, the crowd was on its feet. Straightening out for the run, the ten furlongs having been clocked in 2:04 1/5, Arcaro asked his colt for all he had and kept him on the inside. But The Dancer, remaining on the outside route, the path that had been so successful before the Derby, poked his head in front with a furlong to go. Although his stride appeared to shorten a bit, he held Jamie K. safe by a neck.

His time of 2:28 3/5 tied Middleground's in 1950 as the second-quickest Belmont ever, despite the slow early fractions, and was just two ticks off Citation's and Count Fleet's stakes record. Moreover, he was individually clocked running each of the last four quarters in less than twenty-five seconds, something that neither Count Fleet nor Citation, or even Bolingbroke, while setting the track and American record of 2:27 3/5, had done. In fact, his final two quarters, :24 4/5 and :24 2/5, led George Ryall to comment, "I believe it was Ed Bradley who used to say that a colt that could run the last quarter of a mile-and-a-quarter race in better than 25 seconds was something extra, or words to that effect. Well, Native Dancer ran the last quarter of a mile-and-a-half race in :24 2/5."

Evan Shipman was of the opinion that Native Dancer had just given the most impressive performance of his career. "...that finish in the Belmont

Stakes," he wrote in the 1955 *American Racing Manual*, "was probably not really as close as the distance separating the winner from his runner-up would seem to suggest. Most of us who saw that race were convinced that Native Dancer deliberately cut that finish line, while we also felt that the race proved this son of Polynesian capable of negotiating any distance the American turf demands of a thoroughbred." [3]

Thoroughbred Record columnist Neville Dunn was convinced. "Jamie K. could not have beaten Native Dancer in the Belmont (or the Preakness) if he had all eternity to try for such a feat...I am now content and confident in the belief that this powerful, magnificent gray colt is one of the greatest horses I have ever seen perform on an American race track," he wrote. [4]

Even Arcaro agreed. "I had him for sure," he said after the unsaddling. "Then he got that neck on me, and I just couldn't get by him. If we go around again, Native Dancer's still not gonna let me get past him."

The $82,500 purse carried his earnings over the half-million mark and to ninth on the money earnings list with $522,745.

Native Dancer's next start was the July 4 Dwyer

Stakes at Aqueduct, and Eric Guerin was probably more thankful than usual to be aboard. His mount in the second race had reared in the gate and flipped leaving the jockey shaken up but unharmed. Also earlier on the card, his friend Teddy Atkinson's mount bolted, ran into the fence, and was killed, Atkinson just missing serious injury.

But any nerves Guerin might have had disappeared once he had the gray under him. As for the Dwyer's sixty-fifth running, it was one of those Native Dancer shows that some loved, some didn't. But he ran as a solid 1-20 choice, taking an earlier lead than usual and galloping out the rest of the ten furlongs, without urging, to beat a so-so field in 2:05 1/5.

The fans were disappointed that Jamie K., winner of the June 20 Leonard Richards Stakes at nine furlongs, hadn't been made eligible for the Dwyer and waited anxiously for a rematch in the Arlington Classic in two weeks. Main interest, however, was on a showdown meeting with a horse named Tom Fool.

In the midst of a sweltering heat wave, Native Dancer's arrival in Chicago on July 12 drove the White Sox's battle with the Yankees for the American League lead right off the front page of the sports section. A large, emotional crowd met him at the train station, and one could attribute what happened to emotions, or heat. Walker was leading The Dancer down the ramp when the colt stepped on a piece of cardboard and reared. Two grown men raced for the cardboard and fought over its possession.

The rains that fell on Saturday, July 18, offered a welcome respite and added to the mood that had taken on the sinister overtones of a government coup. The word around Arlington Park was that The Dancer was going to be upset. The track was a quagmire, and the gray, carrying 126 pounds, had to give his seven rivals six pounds. Forget that romp in the Withers at a mile, he was meeting much better horses today. Jamie K.'s trainer, John Partridge, was confident. "With six pounds pull, we definitely will win..."

And from Harold Simmons, conditioner of Van Crosby, "I think I've got everything in my favor against Native Dancer. Six pounds is a lot of weight in such a race. My horse is fresh...The Dancer has been campaigned hard, and it is no secret that he has a pair of ankles that have been viewed with suspicion.

"Also, I'm sure the gray will find Arlington's track

far from his liking. Most of the Eastern courses are of the sandy type. This is hard, solid footing."

The capacity-plus crowd of nearly 40,000 seemed to have taken the "upset" talk seriously and sent Native Dancer to the gate at only 2-3, his highest odds since the Derby. Jamie K. got the slight nod for second choice over Van Crosby, who had tied Arlington's seven-furlong track record of 1:22 in winning the Warren Wright Memorial on July 4. Royal Bay Gem was sent off the fourth choice. Despite the field of eight, there was no show betting.

Breaking from the mile chute that angled off of turn two, Van Crosby reeled off some good numbers despite the heavy going — :23 2/5, :47 1/5, and 1:11 4/5, while Native Dancer dawdled back in sixth. Around the far turn, Guerin pushed a button; the gray moved to third, then just blew by the frontrunners so quickly he was three lengths on top when he turned the corner. "He had such momentum around the turn," Winfrey recalled years later, "that he was several lengths in front before he realized it."

Native Dancer poured it on. Five lengths. Six. Seven. He won by nine, getting the final quarter in a respectable :26 1/5 in the mud. "I think we could have spotted them 20 pounds the way he ran today," said Guerin. No one argued with him, particularly Eddie Arcaro and John Partridge. Jamie K. never rallied and finished fifth.

During The Dancer's romp down the homestretch, usually stoic veteran scribes were standing in the press box, yelling, "Open him up, Guerin! Open him up!"

Must have been the heat.

CHAPTER 11

"...he is one hell of a horse."

"In the great paddock areas of the track each entrant is saddled beneath a certain tree and his admirers can get close enough to tighten the girth themselves." So wrote longtime racing writer and editor David Alexander about the appeal of Saratoga Racecourse.

Part of Saratoga's mystique has always been the special rapport between the horses and the fans. In the early mornings, one can rub elbows with trainers and watch the horses work, and in the paddock in the afternoons, stand so close to the horse to almost reach right out and touch him. Alexander continued: "Only at Saratoga, and during the brief meetings in the spring and fall at little Keeneland, can you still know racing as it used to be — and always ought to be."

One may wonder about the prudence of it, human

nature being what it is. But Alexander said that horse-men never feared for the safety of their horses. It was a good relationship, for racing and fans. But on August 15, 1953, it nearly backfired. That was the day Native Dancer got "mobbed."

A record crowd of 28,260 turned out for the Travers Stakes that day. And it might have occurred to Winfrey that most of them were gathered around The Dancer. The drawback to such a horse could be that at some point he also belongs to the public.

There were few guards then; everyone was always well-behaved. But as the crowd that day continued to grow, those in front were pushed a little closer to the horse. Finally, the temptation was too great. They reached out and touched him. Tentatively, then bolder when he didn't even flinch. They began patting him; some brassier souls actually pulled some hairs from his tail before the guards regained control. Through it all, The Dancer remained unflappable, then he went out and won the race by five and a half lengths.

"He hasn't a nerve in his entire body," Winfrey often said.

The Travers was little more than a tuneup for the American Derby at Washington Park a week later and was less dramatic than the prior scene in the paddock. The Dancer needed only 2:05 3/5 to get the ten furlongs against four rivals, who were admittedly not the cream of the crop and were getting from six to a dozen pounds from the gray's 126 pounds. The $18,850 purse — far from the million-dollar-plus check of today — moved him past Assault into fourth on the money earner's list.

Eric Guerin was grateful the race was as easy as it was. An hour earlier, he had ridden two-year-old Porterhouse to victory in the Saratoga Special then was disqualified and placed last because of repeated interference with Turn-to in the stretch. Moreover, Henry Moreno claimed Guerin's whip hit his colt during the drive. Guerin wondered whether further action would be taken and whether it would affect the American Derby the following Saturday.

The announcement on Monday that Guerin's ten-day suspension would begin on Tuesday and keep him off the gray for the American Derby hit him hard. "I almost cried," he said years later. "It wasn't the money; it was just the great thrill of riding him." [1]

Before leaving for Chicago, Bill Winfrey gave

Vanderbilt the names of the two jockeys he recommended for the American Derby: Teddy Atkinson, one of the country's top riders, and Eddie Arcaro. Then he and Native Dancer left New York on board the Empire State Express. Winfrey personally preferred Arcaro, but he was committed to ride Jamie K. For all his occasional tirades, the Cincinnati, Ohio, native was as good a rider as ever put feet in stirrups. He was particularly talented when it came to handling strong, willful horses, and his ability to judge pace was downright uncanny.

All along the Empire's route, thousands of fans greeted the train wherever it stopped and the door to Native Dancer's car was opened so they could see him. In some areas, fans stood by the tracks and waved. Old-timers said it was reminiscent of the whistle-stop tours the great harness horse Dan Patch made after the turn of the century.

Native Dancer arrived at Washington Park on the Tuesday after the Travers. The next day Arcaro was named his rider for the American Derby when Jamie K. was scratched. "I feel honored to have the mount on Native Dancer," Arcaro told the press. "It's quite a spot to be on, but a nice one at that."

But Dancer fans were horrified. No sooner had the announcement been made than Vanderbilt and Winfrey began receiving telegrams and phone calls pleading with them not to use Arcaro. The jockey had made some harsh remarks earlier in the season about Native Dancer. But Winfrey never had any doubts. "Arcaro was the jockey to get," he said years later. "He was the best rider for the job."

Early on Thursday morning, Eddie Arcaro finally met the horse he had been chasing for two years.

The media arrived at Native Dancer's stall before daylight and bided their time talking with Les Murray until Winfrey, then Arcaro, appeared. Right away the attention put a frown on Arcaro's face. When someone asked him to smile, he said it was too early. He was glad when he was finally legged up. There is sanctuary on a horse's back.

Winfrey asked him to do a "mediocre five" [furlongs] in 1:05, and gallop out another furlong. This was no more than a 'get-acquainted' meeting, but the news coverage resembled that at Louisville. Even Washington Park came to a standstill. The racing secretary's office, usually busy this time of morning, was deserted. Exercise riders pulled their mounts to the sidelines to watch. It's said the outside fence was lined for a quarter of a mile along the backstretch with track people and the press.

Arcaro took The Dancer five furlongs in exactly 1:05, showing why Winfrey wanted him. After dismounting, the thirty-seven year old turned his attention to the media, which besieged him with questions. He said the hype was "so silly to me. I just can't see this big build-up. All I've done is exercise him and now I'm being asked what I think about him as a racehorse. Well, he's a powerful animal, for sure, and he handled well and has a good disposition. I once said he didn't look all that sound to me, but I have to say, he looks good now. Mr. Winfrey says his ankles are back to normal size. They look it to me."

"How does he compare with others you've ridden?"

"Citation is the greatest horse I've ever ridden," he snapped. "It's foolish to try to compare them. Even if I win on him, you can't compare horses after just one ride. I don't care to comment any further. I'll be riding him on Saturday." [2]

Arcaro knew all along his ride on Native Dancer was

an unpopular one, but he wasn't prepared for the hostility that greeted him at the paddock. "Listen Arcaro, that horse better win or else!" someone yelled among the heckling and boos. Stone-faced, he listened to Winfrey, and moments later the eight starters took to the track for the forty-third American Derby before a near-record crowd of 37,108 fans. Arcaro concentrated on riding the colt. *Seems like all Eric has to do is push a button*, he thought to himself. *Just like driving a car. Citation was like that.*

It was a decent field getting eight to fourteen pounds: Sir Mango, sharp winner of a mile prep at the track; Hasty House Farm's stakes-winning duo of Stan and Platan; and Landlocked, winner of the Choice Stakes and Lamplighter Handicap. Native Dancer carried 128 pounds, attempting to become the first to win with more than 126 in a 'who's who' of winners that included Cavalcade, Whirlaway, Alsab, Citation, and Ponder. The gray and his stablemate, Beachcomber, went off at 1-5, and, yet again, no show betting was allowed.

Arcaro's hopes of an uneventful trip were dashed at the start. Lacking anything that resembled early speed,

The Dancer had only one horse beaten after going a quarter-mile, nine and a half lengths off Sir Mango's pace. After another quarter, he was still seventh, more than ten lengths out of first. Arcaro began to scrub vigorously, and the gray advanced to fourth with six of the nine furlongs remaining. After posting fractions of :22 3/5, :46 2/5, and 1:10 3/5, Sir Mango hit the mile in 1:35 2/5 and then began to fall apart. Down Washington Park's 1,531-foot long stretch, The Dancer still had three horses to beat. Arcaro felt his fingers tighten around the whip.

He wouldn't need it. Native Dancer flattened his ears, lengthened his stride, and made the lead with a sixteenth to go. He drew clear to win with plenty left in the tank. Winning by two lengths, his time for the nine furlongs, 1:48 2/5, was only a tick off of Colosal's track record, and he had run the final quarter in twenty-three seconds.

Arcaro regained his composure by the time he arrived in the winner's circle, but his stomach felt like he was still on a roller coaster. "He handled himself perfectly," he said, managing a smile. "But going down the backstretch he didn't seem to be doing too much.

Nearing the half mile pole, I got busy and started to 'pump' on him. He still didn't do much, but all of a sudden he started to run and that was it. Apparently this horse likes to make his move when he sees fit.

"After riding the Dancer today I can say that the big gray is one of the greatest horses I have ever been aboard...he is just one hell of a horse." [3]

"He's everything they've said about him," Joe Estes quoted Arcaro in the *American Race Horses of 1953*. "But that dude had me worried down the backstretch."

Al Popara was riding at Washington Park that day and was in the jockeys' dressing room when Arcaro came in, undressed, and threw his silks down. "Here I am riding one of the best horses in the country, who only got beat once in his life, and then Guerin got criticized [sic] for it. Who is odds on favorite, and he scared the hell out of me. I moved at the 3/8th pole and he moved at the 1/4 pole. This horse is smarter than I am — he knows when to make his move," Arcaro told his fellow rider.

The Dancer impressed a good many observers, among them *The Blood-Horse*'s Frank Butzow. "Through the years since 1884, there have been occasions when the American Derby was won with consummate ease...But, no previous winner [including Boundless, Whirlaway, and Alsab] captured Chicago's famous race with greater facility than Native Dancer. His margin of victory...may have been narrower than those of some of his predecessors, but none was more impressive in achievement."

The $66,500 purse boosted Native Dancer's earnings to $743,920. A combination of any two or three of the rich fall races could put him in third behind Stymie's $918,485 second-place earnings on the money earners list. Except for the prestigious Lawrence Realization at a mile and five-eighths, there was nothing left to prove in his division. His main goal now was to meet Greentree Stable's four-year-old Tom Fool, whose recent victories in the Wilson and Whitney Stakes ran his awesome season to eight wins without a loss. The son of Menow either had to reverse form dramatically in his remaining starts, or The Dancer was going to have to put him away for Horse of the Year.

However, neither owner was interested in a match race. To lure both Native Dancer and Tom Fool, the Westchester Racing Association announced they would increase the Sysonby Stakes purse of $20,000 by some $30,000 and move the date up from October 6 to September 26. Not to be outdone, the Maryland Jockey Club doubled the purse of the Pimlico Special to be run on October 24. The Sysonby's date change compromised running in the Lawrence Realization, but, said Winfrey, "When they go from twenty thousand to fifty thousand, I'm going to make my plans coincide with theirs."

However, the two stars would not meet.

Through the bucked shins, the osselets, and the big ankles over the past two years, Native Dancer had never taken a bad step. But during the first week of September, he returned from a workout favoring his left front foot. Veterinarian William Wright found four bruises, one containing pus, which he pared. The Dancer breezed on September 10, after which Dr. Wright reported the bruises hadn't healed enough to stand serious work for a week. With the Sysonby only two weeks off, Native Dancer was scratched. Tom Fool won it by three lengths. Only one start remained on Tom Fool's schedule before retirement — the Pimlico Special.

When Native Dancer favored the foot yet again following a gallop, Dr. Wright found two new festered bruises. On Saturday, September 19, Vanderbilt announced that Native Dancer was through for the year. The colt would go to Sagamore, where the decision would be made on racing him at four.

Tom Fool nailed Horse of the Year with an easy victory in the Pimlico Special.

NATIVE DANCER

CHAPTER 12

From Boy Into Man

As Native Dancer recovered at Sagamore over the winter, sacks of get-well cards and fan mail, most addressed to him personally, poured into Alfred Vanderbilt's New York City office. Vanderbilt himself, in the meantime, was handling the joys and disappointments of horse racing with his usual wit. When he was honored before the Thoroughbred Club of America, he closed his speech telling his hosts he would remember the honor with pride:

"Maybe it would be a greater thrill to win the Kentucky Derby. I wouldn't know about that. But one thing I do know for sure — this beats running second."

Supervised by Ralph Kercheval, Native Dancer was galloped daily under tack. By January, he was going a mile and a half every day. As time neared for his return to competition, tracks across the country increased their purses in hopes of attracting him. But Vanderbilt already had his 1954 campaign pretty well mapped out, including a trip to Paris to run in the Prix de l'Arc de Triomphe at Longchamp.

His immediate objectives were the Metropolitan, Brooklyn, and Suburban Handicaps — the "Handicap Triple Crown." And there was the Whitney Handicap, Saratoga Cup, and Pimlico Special, concluding with the two-mile Jockey Club Gold Cup.

When Native Dancer returned to Belmont in late March, the press got its first look at the four-year-old. He was much lighter in color now, and although he had put on a couple hundred pounds, there wasn't a hint of flab, thanks to Kercheval's daily work schedule. Native Dancer had, in fact, so toned up that he resembled a statue chiseled in light gray granite. It was as though he had been a work in progress for the past two years and now was "a finished product...the muscular front-end fully complemented by a strong mid-section and powerful quarters," wrote Timothy Capps in the *Mid-Atlantic Thoroughbred*. "He had the explosive muscularity of a sprinter and the balance and tremendous stride of a stayer. In short, he was a presence."

Evan Shipman, writing in the *American Racing Manual*, predicted that Native Dancer's sprinter-stayer "length and leanness" would someday be the standard for "the American horse." Close to 16.3 hands high, The Dancer was a "thoroughbred of exceptional size and scope, and every ounce of that noble physique was animated with the energy of a dynamo...Native Dancer combined his great strength with rare intelligence." [1]

Not that he wasn't still impish, said Pat O' Brien in *The Blood-Horse* of May 15, 1954, he was just "not so devilishly juvenile about it." He was like the boy who joined the army and came home a man.

Native Dancer debuted May 7 in the six-furlong Commando Purse at Belmont, sent off at 1-6 by a Friday crowd of nearly 22,000. The only excitement involved a delay in the saddling while Bill Winfrey looked for a larger girth. Otherwise, The Dancer, carrying 126 pounds and giving such seasoned handicappers as Alerted and Combat Boots up to thirteen pounds, made short work of the race. It was far easier than the one-and-a-quarter-length winning margin would indicate. His time of 1:11 4/5 was little more than a good workout for the mile Metropolitan Handicap on May 15.

The next day, Greentree Stable's Straight Face won the Dixie Handicap at Pimlico, covering the nine furlongs in 1:51, four-fifths of a second off the track record. No one could recall the Count Fleet gelding ever looking better. John Campbell, racing secretary and handicapper for the New York tracks, agreed and increased his impost by two pounds to 117 for the Metropolitan. Native Dancer would tote 130, the same weight Tom Fool carried the year before.

Bob Horwood, who had been reluctant to join The Dancer's fan club in 1953, admitted to changing his mind. Writing in the *Thoroughbred Record* of May 22, 1954, he said, "...I must confess to having rarely been so thoroughly convinced as I was by my first long view of Native Dancer this year." But he was just as impressed by Straight Face and warned if the latter "...is able to run his best race for Ted Atkinson...only a great horse can give him thirteen pounds and a beating."

Encouraged by Native Dancer's impost and weight concessions of up to twenty-four pounds, eight owners sent their hopefuls out to test him in the sixty-first renewal of the Metropolitan. About 3,000 fans ignored watching 1953 juvenile champion Porterhouse beat older horses in the Knickerbocker Handicap, and instead, elected to watch the gray be saddled. The Dancer rewarded his fans' loyalty by rearing when Winfrey tightened the girth. "Look at him," someone yelled. "He knows he's the champ."

The crowd sent him off at 1-4, with Straight Face the obvious second choice at 7.30-1. Right out of the starting gate, set up on the backstretch, Straight Face took the initiative and went to the front. After a quarter, Native Dancer was next to last and eight lengths back, while Straight Face reeled off :23 1/5 for the first quarter-mile and :22 4/5 for the next, a track-record pace. Atkinson managed to slow him down to :24 1/5, his six-furlong time of 1:10 1/5 only two ticks off the track record. Native Dancer in the meantime had moved to fifth at that point, seven lengths off the leader.

At the top of the stretch, Straight Face had three and a half lengths on Impasse and appeared to be running as strong as ever. At the point where the Widener Course entered the main track, Native Dancer was in second and still had more than three lengths to make up. A sharp eye would see that Straight Face was beginning to lose some steam, but it still seemed that the gray had more track to make up than Straight Face was losing in velocity. "Straight Face was out there, sailing," said Winfrey years later, "...and he was pretty damn good. Turning for home...it looked like an impossible task, because Straight Face wasn't coming back." [2]

Native Dancer fans were heartsick. For those who had seen the Derby, it felt like déjà vu. But with Native Dancer, the difficult was easy; the impossible just took a little longer. Eric Guerin felt the power shifting under him; something, he said, that was difficult to describe. The Dancer's stride lengthened. He lowered his head and flattened his ears. A few yards out, the Gray Ghost caught Greentree's runner, and in one great lunge shoved his neck in front. His time, 1:35 1/5, was only two ticks off of Count Fleet's track record, one tick off the stakes record, and three quicker than Tom Fool's the year before.

"Was I scared?" Guerin's voice quivered. "You're damned right — right down to 50 yards away." [3]

"This traditional feature," Joe Hirsch wrote, "...has had some storied renewals but the 1954 edition must rank with the finest races of the century. Anyone who witnessed it will never forget The Dancer's performance." [4]

Hirsch had lost none of the excitement when this writer talked to him in early 2000. "It was electrifying! He flew by those horses...it was just glorious! Everything horse racing is meant to be."

On Monday, May 24, The Dancer turned in a good mile workout, then took a bad step. X-rays were negative. The next morning, Native Dancer walked for an hour without a limp. Anxious reporters were told the Suburban Handicap was still a go.

On Wednesday, he was reshod and galloped riderless for two miles with no distress. That same day, John Campbell posted his weights for the Suburban: Native Dancer, 133 pounds; Straight Face, 118.

The next day, Native Dancer worked three furlongs in :36 2/5 and pulled up lame with Bernie Everson dismounting on the track. Dr. Wright's diagnosis: "a bruised digital cushion with a secondary inflammation of the bursae between the coffin bone and navicular bone." [5] The horse was scratched from the Suburban.

Straight Face showed he was a solid and versatile

handicap horse when he came from well off the pace to win the Suburban by four and a half lengths.

The dog days of summer found Native Dancer back at Saratoga with that ambitious schedule of races ahead of him, including the Whitney Handicap and Saratoga Cup. He had been brought along slowly over the summer, from wearing bar plates during slow gallops to a steel shoe with a clipped toe when more serious works began.

The Dancer was more popular than ever at The Spa. On mornings he worked out, the breakfast tables on the clubhouse veranda were jammed, and all activity came to a stop. Caterer Frank Stevens said, "There hasn't been anything like it since Man o' War's time here."

Finally on Wednesday, August 11, The Dancer went seven furlongs in 1:26 3/5 under a strong hold. He was ready. So on a dark and rainy Monday five days later, he went to the post in the Oneonta, a seven-furlong overnight handicap. John Campbell had passed away over the summer and his successor, Frank E. (Jimmy) Kilroe, handed the gray 137 pounds, while his two opponents, stablemate First Glance and J. W. Brown's Gigantic, received eighteen and thirty pounds, respectively. Because of the small field, there was no betting.

A real "frog-strangler" of a rain and hailstorm hit Saratoga twenty minutes before post time. In spite of walking an obstacle course of water puddles, ice pellets, and broken twigs, hundreds of fans gathered around the Dutch elm in the southeast corner of the paddock to watch The Dancer being saddled. Wearing the broadest grin of anybody was Les Murray. He was sixty-five on this day and celebrated by walking his beloved "bum" over from the barn himself.

The track was ankle deep in mud. Native Dancer had won on off tracks before, but not carrying this kind of weight. However, with the way he ran, he could have carried 140 pounds or more. He went around First Glance on the far turn and never looked back to win by nine lengths in a respectable 1:24 4/5, less than two seconds slower than the track standard. Winfrey wanted a brisk mile, so the gray hummed along another furlong to get the mile in 1:38.

Kilroe's weights for Saturday's Whitney disappointed Vanderbilt. Not that he didn't think his colt could carry 136 pounds, but coming just five days after the Oneonta wasn't fair to the horse. So he scratched him.

The next objective was the Saratoga Cup at a mile and three-quarters on August 27.

Vanderbilt did have a Whitney starter, however — Social Outcast won handily.

On Sunday morning, August 22, Native Dancer worked a mile and three-eighths in 2:24 3/5. Ten minutes later he went lame in the right front foot. The veterinarian checked the foot and conferred with Winfrey, who conferred with Vanderbilt. The latter was on a lunch break from the annual meeting of The Jockey Club Conference on Racing Matters. After he and his twenty-three colleagues filed back into Saratoga's President's Room, Vanderbilt reached for a note pad and on the top sheet wrote, ND NG. He then tore it off and handed it to Robert Fulton Kelley, publicity director for the New York tracks.

Kelley's face drained of color. ND NG — Native Dancer No Good.

A short time later, Vanderbilt issued this statement to the news media:

"After working out this morning, Native Dancer showed a recurrence of his former injury. There appears to be no other choice but to retire him from racing. He will not race again and will enter stud at Sagamore Farm in Maryland next spring."

On October 2, Les Murray braided The Dancer's mane for the last time. Then Murray, dressed in a new red checkered hat and shirt, along with Hal Walker, led the gray to the paddock. Bill Winfrey quietly saddled him and gave Eric Guerin, dressed in full silks, a boost up. With Bernie Everson on a lead pony, The Dancer began his last walk to the track prior to the Woodward Stakes. In a ripple effect, the applause began in the paddock and spread to the grandstand. When The Gray Ghost stepped onto the Belmont surface, the crowd gave him a standing ovation.

Race caller Fred Capossela introduced him then respectfully shut off the mike. With Guerin standing in the irons, The Dancer bowed his head and cantered to the head of the stretch, where he was turned around and given some slack. More than 30,000 spectators continued to stand and cheer. The Gray Ghost obliged and ran fifty yards beyond the finish line before Guerin could haul him in. One last trip to the winner's circle, where Belmont's president, George Widener Jr., presented Vanderbilt with a silver plaque engraved with

The Dancer's name and accomplishments. Then it was all over.

At daybreak three days later, a van pulled up to Barn 20 at Belmont Park. Wearing his leather hat, a light blanket, and leg wraps, The Dancer was led from his stall. He paused at the ramp as though remembering scenes of his greatest victories — the Futurity, the Belmont Stakes, and that impossible run in the Metropolitan Handicap. Finally, Native Dancer followed Les Murray up the ramp and into the van.

Bill Winfrey slapped him on the rump and said, "So long. Have a good trip."

CHAPTER 13

"A Horse of the Ages"

Native Dancer was voted the year's best horse in all polls.

Of his championship season, Charles Hatton wrote in the *American Racing Manual*: "A champion — hailed rather than merely acknowledged — in each of his three seasons in competition, Native Dancer was voted Horse of the Year in 1954…nobody with the vaguest knowledge of form questioned he was the classiest performer in training, and many regard the marvelous gray as a Horse of the Ages…" [1]

In 1958, Native Dancer's first two-year-olds hit the track. On April 19 of that year, his son East Indian caught the public's attention when he paraded to the post at Jamaica for his first start. A small bay colt, East Indian bore no resemblance to his famous sire, but otherwise, the circumstances were almost eerie. It was six years to the day that Native Dancer made his debut.

The track, distance, jockey, weight were all the same: Jamaica, five furlongs, Eric Guerin, 118 pounds. He was even the race's favorite. And he won by two and a quarter lengths. Said Guerin afterward, "It's the biggest thrill I've had since his daddy retired."

East Indian also won his second start, an allowance at Saratoga, but here the resemblance ends. Owned by Circle M Farm and trained by C. W. Parish, he ran primarily in allowance and claiming events through the age of six, with only one stakes placing, a third in the 1958 Grand Union Hotel Stakes at Saratoga.

The best runner from Native Dancer's first crop was Mrs. Peter Widener's Dan Cupid, winner of several French stakes. Dan Cupid sired the great Sea-Bird in his first crop (1962) and was France's second leading sire in 1965. Sea-Bird lost only once in his career and won at distances to a mile and a half, including the Epsom Derby and the Prix de l'Arc de Triomphe.

Most of the top gallopers from The Dancer's first few crops were European-raced fillies, including Secret Step and the smashing Hula Dancer. Champion two-year-old of France in 1962, Hula Dancer lost only once, was never beaten by males, and won from sprints to ten furlongs.

One filly from his second crop (1957) didn't do much on the racetrack, but her first foal brought her fame and Native Dancer to prominence as a broodmare sire. Owned by Canadian horseman Edward P. Taylor, Natalma won three of seven starts altogether and was disqualified for interference in the Spinaway, the only stakes in which she finished first. Injured in training at three, she was retired and bred the same year to six-year-old Nearctic, a Canadian Horse of the Year. The result of this union was a bay colt with a striking blaze and three white feet wrapped up in a compact package called Northern Dancer.

Barely topping 15.1 hands while racing, Northern Dancer was an outstanding runner, winning fourteen of his eighteen starts, including the Flamingo, Blue Grass, and Florida Derby. The second choice at Louisville, he won the 1964 Kentucky Derby in 2:00, a record that stood until Secretariat's 1:59 2/5 in 1973. He also won the Preakness, ran third in the Belmont, then smashed the Queen's Plate at the Ontario track, Woodbine, by seven and a half lengths to end his career. He was Canada's Horse of the Year and the United States' champion three-year-old.

There aren't enough superlatives to describe Northern Dancer's stud career. From just his first crop (1966) came champions Viceregal and Dance Act; from his second, champions Nijinsky II, winner of the 1970 English Triple Crown, and Fanfreluche. And so on. He became the first North American-based stallion to get 100 stakes winners. By the time he died in November of 1990, he had sired 143 stakes winners and twenty-six champions in both North America and England. (His lifetime total is 146 stakes winners.)

As for Native Dancer, his first really top-class American runner, Raise a Native, came from the same 1961 crop that produced Atan, whose son Sharpen Up sired a multitude of good European runners, including Diesis, Pebbles, and Trempolino. Raise a Native's career was brief but brilliant. Louis Wolfson paid $39,000 for him at the 1962 Saratoga yearling sale, and the bright chestnut won all four starts in 1963, setting new Aqueduct standards for five furlongs (:57 4/5), then five and a half furlongs (1:02 3/5) in the Great American Stakes, and equaling his five-furlong time in the Juvenile. An injury sustained while training for the Sapling Stakes ended Raise a Native's career, yet he was voted the juvenile champion and topped the Experimental Free Handicap with 126 pounds.

Wolfson was disappointed. He had bought the colt in hopes of winning the next year's classics. "One of these days, we'll grab onto another one," he said.[2] Indeed he did. In 1974, Wolfson bred his mare Won't Tell You to Exclusive Native, one of Raise a Native's best-producing sons. The result was an elegant chestnut named Affirmed. He won the 1978 Triple Crown and became one of the all-time great runners. (Incidentally, Alydar, the only horse to finish second in all three races, was a son of Raise a Native.) Raise a Native's legacy could fill a book.

The first Native Dancer offspring to get to the classics was Native Charger. He finished fourth in both the 1965 Derby and Preakness, but sired High Echelon, winner of the 1970 Belmont Stakes. Native Dancer's daughter, Shenanigans, from the 1963 crop, produced only six foals, but half of them were stakes winners: Icecapade, Buckfinder, and the ill-fated Ruffian. She can be found in the pedigrees of too many to list, but they include Afternoon Deelites, Coronado's Quest, Preakness winner Louis Quatorze, Sultry Song, and so on. Shenanigans was named the 1975 Broodmare of the Year.

From the same crop as Shenanigans came the first Native Dancer son to avenge his sire. When a reporter asked Dr. Frank O'Keefe why he sent his mare Sweep In to Native Dancer, he replied, "...because I thought he was the greatest competitive race horse I had ever seen." [3] The result of this union was a dark brown colt named Kauai King.

Michael Ford paid $42,000 for the Maryland-bred at the 1964 Saratoga yearling sale. Kauai King won once in four juvenile starts and carried a three-race winning streak, including the Fountain of Youth Stakes into the 1966 Kentucky Derby. The crowd made him the 2.40-1 favorite over fourteen rivals. Despite fractions of :22 4/5, :46 1/5, 1:10 3/5, and 1:35 — no horse had ever posted 1:35 and won — Kauai King turned back four challengers, including Advocator in a stretch-long battle to win the Derby by a half-length in 2:02, the same time as Dark Star. With Native Street winning the Kentucky Oaks the day before, Kauai King's victory gave their sire a rare Oaks/Derby double. Kauai King won the Preakness, but was rank in the Belmont Stakes. He tired and finished fourth. His career ended soon after with a pulled suspensory in his left foreleg.

Two years later, a small gray colt with a dark smudge in the middle of his face also arrived at Churchill Downs off a three-race winning streak and a growing fan base. When he had caught Iron Ruler inside the sixteenth-pole to win the Wood Memorial then survived a foul claim, some 55,000 Aqueduct fans roared their approval, some weeping. Native Dancer had passed away just months earlier; what could be better than for another son to win the Derby — one with the name of Dancer's Image?

Bred by Peter Fuller, a Boston Cadillac dealer with seven children, Dancer's Image was foaled at Sagamore Farm in 1965. When the colt was a yearling, Fuller's trainer Lou Cavalaris didn't like the looks of his ankles and recommended selling him. Reluctantly, Fuller consigned him to the Florida Breeders' Sales Company auction at Hialeah. He took along his wife, Joan, who liked this little guy and hated to see him go. So, as the bidding neared $25,000, she nudged her husband. Had he noticed how alert the colt was? And strong looking? Then — the coup de grace — "He's so neat." That did it. For $26,000, Peter Fuller again owned the colt with the suspicious ankles.[4]

Dancer's Image was a sturdy juvenile, starting fifteen times and winning eight, seven in Canada and the Maryland Futurity in the United States.

While in residence at Churchill Downs before the Derby, he was treated by well-known equine veterinarian Dr. Alex Harthill. One of the drugs he gave the colt was phenylbutazone (Bute), an anti-inflammatory drug that was legal in Kentucky at the time only if it didn't show up in the post-race testing. Harthill gave him Bute on April 28, allowing six days for the drug to clear from the colt's system.

On Derby morning, Dancer's Image stood with his ankles in ice, then went out in Fuller's green and gold silks and a bright yellow shadow roll to defeat Calumet Farm's Forward Pass. But the wildly popular victory was short-lived, for Dancer's Image was disqualified after testing positive for Bute. Forward Pass was moved up to first, taking the $122,600 main prize.

Many fans believed the colt had been "robbed." Even the late Turf historian and writer Jim Bolus painted the jockey statue in his yard in Fuller's colors "in honor," he said, "of the horse and the man who had the Derby taken away from them." [5]

The hard-luck colt had his number moved again in the

Preakness, this time from third to eighth for bothering horses in the stretch. Training for the Belmont, Dancer's Image came out of a workout sore and was retired.

Fuller waged an ultimately unsuccessful five-year legal battle to clear his horse's name. Like a scarlet letter, Dancer's Image will forever bear an asterisk by his name.

Dancer's Image's stud career spanned the globe, from Glade Valley Farms in Maryland to Killeen Castle Stud in Ireland, three seasons in France, and finally to Japan in 1979. Of his thirty-one stakes winners, Dancer's Image sired several top sprinters in Europe, including Lianga, the 1975 French champion.

In 2000, thirty-three years after his death, Native Dancer's blood still dominates the sport and particularly the classics, as evidenced by the 2000 Kentucky Derby win of Fusaichi Pegasus, a great-grandson through Mr. Prospector. Other classic connections include Majestic Prince, a grandson through Raise a Native, who in 1969 became the first unbeaten winner of both the Derby and Preakness; Genuine Risk, a great-granddaughter who in 1980 became only the second filly, and the first in sixty-five years, to win the Derby; great-grandsons Alysheba, who captured the Derby and Preakness in 1987, and Strike the Gold, who won the Derby in 1991; and great-great grandson Unbridled, the 1991 Derby winner. More recent tail male descendants who have won the Derby include Thunder Gulch (1995), Grindstone (1996), and Real Quiet (1998).

Native Dancer may have lost the Derby, but as respected Turf writer Edward L. Bowen observed in *The Great Ones*, " 'The Ghost' took up residence at Churchill Downs, where it has exerted unusual influence."

Twenty-five years after The Dancer's death, Tony Morris of England's *Racing Post* wrote that, "it would be no exaggeration to call him the most influential sire of the second half of the twentieth century."

Morris concluded that Native Dancer "is right up there among the leaders of the Premier League, with such as Nearco, Hyperion and precious few others for company."

NATIVE DANCER

EPILOGUE

"For the great, death dies."

Native Dancer arrived at Sagamore on October 5, 1954, to a bevy of photographers, reporters, and a CBS television crew. The first thing he did, like a movie horse on cue, was rear. Then, he was led around for the picture takers, during which he stopped and examined his surroundings. The smells, the sounds, they were all familiar. But they had never stirred him up so before.

In the stallion barn, The Dancer was put into the number one stall, occupied for nearly two decades by Discovery. The twenty-three year old stallion, the patriarch and foundation of Sagamore, was forced to abdicate his reign. He kept his old paddock, however, since it was his "territory."

It didn't take Native Dancer long to regard his paddock as his own territory, one to defend to the death against any dangerous threat.

"He wouldn't even let a bird land in the paddock," groom Joe Hall said. "If he saw one sit on the ground...he charged the bird. Even ones sitting on the fence."

But the sturdiest of fences ultimately gives in to 1,300 pounds of brute force, so a strand of electric wire was run along the top board. It didn't work.

"He fought that thing! Every time he'd run at it, it'd shock him but he'd still run back to attack it," said Hall.[1]

Eventually Native Dancer was satisfied that the matter of his rank had been settled.

He was still an unusually powerful stallion, and Hall knew there was an element of danger around him. But the groom loved him. "Oh, gawd, he was a lovely horse when he was stirred up."[2]

Native Dancer tested everyone who handled him to see who he could intimidate. Ralph Kercheval remembers the time the gray tested him. "He was always wanting to rear when I led him out. So one day I said, 'It's you or me, buddy,' and gave a hard yank on the shank. He reared so high he fell over backwards and hit the ground like a ton of bricks. I was scared to death; he could have broken his back. But he got up and came right on over to me and behaved like a gentleman from then on."

The Dancer was especially rough on grooms. "His first groom was Henry Farman," said Hall, who became head stallion groom in 1959. "Dancer bit off one of his fingers. Second groom was Hogan Williams. Dancer bit his arm.

"Trouble with those fellows was they didn't respect him. They went into the paddock to catch him. Me, I always waited on him at the gate. I took a carrot with me every time. I'd call to him, hold up the carrot and wait...he'd run round and round. Once I had to wait an hour and a half 'fore I could get a shank on. Usually, though, it'd only take a few minutes...Once you got aholt of him he was a gentleman." [3] Hall said that in a lifetime of rubbing horses, he became attached to only two: Discovery and Native Dancer.

Discovery had been retired from stud duty not long after The Dancer's arrival. By 1958 he was spending more and more of his time under a tree in his paddock. He didn't run anymore and walked as little as possible. Mrs. Kercheval explained that he had foundered when he was younger and his feet bothered him after that. Now the pain was getting too bad. In late August of 1958, Kercheval and Vanderbilt bid their beloved "Pops" goodbye and left Sagamore for a few days.

"It broke Ralph's heart," she said. "He told them, 'wait until I'm not here.' "

They did. Discovery was put down the next day.

In 1961, Native Dancer suffered an attack of colic. Having never raced on medications of any kind, he was extraordinarily fit and recovered quickly. So when he came down with colic again six years later, everyone expected him to snap through it as well.

Shortly before noon on Tuesday, November 14, 1967, Hall went out to bring him in from the paddock. The seventeen-year-old stallion was white now, just a shade darker in his mane and tail.

"Pretty soon he ambled over," said Hall, "and I put the shank on him." Then the fifty-three-year-old groom offered him the carrot but Native Dancer refused it. "Thought he just didn't want no carrot." Hall led him to his stall and again offered the treat. This time, The Dancer turned his head and touched his side. "That's when I knew my horse wasn't right."

Hall quickly summoned Noah Gill, the breeding stock supervisor. Gill dosed him with two ounces of "colic medicine," then telephoned Sagamore's veterinarian, Dr. I. W. Frock, and notified Harold Ferguson,

Sagamore's manager since Kercheval had resigned in 1959. Ferguson called Vanderbilt.

The next twenty-two hours were a roller-coaster ride. The Dancer would improve after a dose, then slide. But after examining him on Wednesday morning, Frock recommended surgery, as the horse likely had a blockage. Ferguson rang Vanderbilt, who told him to get the horse to the New Bolton Veterinary Center at the University of Pennsylvania, one of the best equine clinics in the country and only about four hours from Sagamore.

Around 6:30 that evening, The Dancer was loaded into the van. Hall, who never left him during the ordeal, rode with him. They arrived at New Bolton shortly after 11 p.m., where Hall said they took him "right into the operating room. They don't waste no time at all. It's an emergency."

The surgery began at 11:30 p.m. Doctors Charles W. Raker, Loren Evans, and Ingemar Norberg removed a tumor that had grown to the abdominal wall, and about ten feet of intestine. Around 2 a.m., Native Dancer was wheeled into a padded recovery room.

Over the next three hours, he was brought out of

the anesthesia slowly, out of the "fight or flight" state in which many horses awaken. But The Dancer calmed rather quickly and was encouraged to stand. Wobbly in his first try, he sat back on his haunches. "All the time I'm talkin' to him," said Hall.

Native Dancer almost made it on his second effort. But suddenly, his once-powerful body slumped to the pad. "I'm standin' beside him," said Hall. "He draws a deep breath and then he don't breathe no more."

It was 5:15 a.m., November 16, 1967.

Although Sagamore had been notified, the place looked vacant when the van, now carrying The Dancer's body, arrived at 11:30 Thursday morning. Hall asked the driver to blow the horn.

"When I hear that horn then all of a sudden I can't hold the water back to save my life. The water runs down my face. I don't know why the horn did that to me. I was sittin' right under it, but it sounds so far away.

"I said to the driver: 'Man, don't blow that horn no more.' " [4]

The whole industry, along with Vanderbilt, mourned the loss of Native Dancer with a flood of eulogies and recollections. "I had more affection and

161

admiration for him than any other horse I ever owned," said Vanderbilt.

The Kerchevals were shocked. "He was very close to me," Ralph Kercheval said in a 1999 interview. "I thought Secretariat's Belmont Stakes was one of the most awesome races of all time, but overall, Native Dancer could have beaten him on any given day."

It isn't unusual for jockeys to form close bonds with their mounts. "It's hard to explain how I felt about that horse," Eric Guerin said. "I used to go to the barn, and I'd watch that gray horse and I'd get a funny feeling in the pit of my stomach. I'm just sorry that every jockey didn't have the chance to ride him so they would all know how magnificent he really was." [5]

Bud Troyer rode The Dancer at Sagamore, keeping him fit with daily two-mile gallops, taking eight circuits of the half-mile training track. "You aren't going to believe this," he enjoyed telling visitors, "...without any indication from me, Native Dancer would stop dead precisely as we completed the eighth lap. He was the most intelligent horse I ever worked with...I loved him. There was never a greater racehorse." [6]

The Gray Ghost was buried intact, next to

Discovery, on a gently sloping hill in the farm's cemetery. Native Dancer's seven-year-old son, Restless Native, inherited his paddock and stall. But for Joe Hall, no other horse could fill them.

"I often go up and stand there [Dancer's grave]," he said in Patrick Robinson's *Classic Lines*. "He may have been the greatest horse of all time. He'd have given any horse in history a race and probably have beaten them all — Man o' War, Secretariat, and the rest — just as long as no one actually told him to do it, just as long as they'd let him do it his way."

In 1963, four years prior to his death, Native Dancer had received his due recognition from the racing industry when he was inducted into the Racing Hall of Fame.

The late Charles Hatton wrote in *Daily Racing Form* that Native Dancer was "one of the few truly great performers in 300 years of American racing...Some have said that 'for the great, death dies.' The Dancer will live on indefinitely in his species."[7]

NATIVE DANCER's
PEDIGREE

		Phalaris
	Sickle, 1924	Selene
Unbreakable, 1935		
		Prince Palatine
	Blue Glass, 1917	Hour Glass II
POLYNESIAN, br, 1942		
		Polymelus
	Polymelian, 1914	Pasquita
	Black Polly, 1936	
		Pompey
	Black Queen, 1930	Black Maria
NATIVE DANCER, gray colt, 1950		
		Fair Play
	Display, 1923	Cicuta
	Discovery, 1931	
		Light Brigade
	Ariadne, 1926	Adrienne
GEISHA, ro, 1943		
		Whisk Broom II
	John P. Grier, 1917	Wonder
	Miyako, 1935	
		Sweep
	La Chica, 1930	La Grisette

NATIVE DANCER's RACE RECORD

Native Dancer — gr. c. 1950, by Polynesian (Unbreakable)–Geisha, by Discovery — **Lifetime record: 22 21 1 0 $785,240**

Own.– A.G. Vanderbilt
Br.– Alfred G. Vanderbilt (Ky)
Tr.– W.C. Winfrey

16Aug54- 0Sar	sly 7f	:23^3 :47^2 1:12 1:24^4	3↑ Handicap 5025	2	3	$2^{2\frac12}$	2^2	1^8	1^9	Guerin E	137	w	-	91-19	Native Dancer137^{9}First Glance119$^{4\frac12}$Gigantic107	Easily	3
15May54- 6Bel	fst 1	:23^1 :46 1:10^1 1:35^1	3↑ Metropolitan H 39k	3	8	$7^{7\frac34}$	5^7	$2^{3\frac12}$	1^{nk}	Guerin E	130	w	*.25	98-11	Native Dancer130^{nk}Straight Face117^{6}Jamie K.110^2	Just up	9
7May54- 6Bel	fst 6f	:22^4 :46^3 1:11^4	3↑ Alw 15000	4	3	4^2	3^1	1^2	$1^{1\frac14}$	Guerin E	126	w	*.15	90-15	Native Dancer126$^{1\frac14}$Laffango121^{nk}Impasse114^{nk}	Easily best	7
22Aug53- 7Was	fst 1⅛	:46^2 1:10^3 1:35^2 1:48^2	American Derby 112k	4	7	7^{11}	$4^{5\frac12}$	$4^{1\frac34}$	1^2	Arcaro E	128	w	*.20e	99-11	NativeDancr128^{2}Landlocked120$^{1\frac14}$PrecousSton114^3	Drew out	8
15Aug53- 6Sar	fst 1¼	:49^4 1:14 1:33^3 2:05^3	Travers 27k	1	3	3^1	$2^{1\frac12}$	1^1	$1^{5\frac12}$	Guerin E	126	w	*.05	80-20	NativeDancer126$^{5\frac12}$Dictar120$^{2\frac12}$GuardianII114^1	Easily best	5
	Geldings not eligible																
18Jly53- 7AP	hy 1	:23^2 :47^1 1:11^4 1:38	Arl Classic 154k	4	6	6^7	3^4	1^3	1^3	Guerin E	126	w	*.70	82-25	NativeDancer126^{9}SirMango120^{hd}VanCrosby120^2	Easily best	8
4Jly53- 6Aqu	fst 1¼	:49^4 1:14 1:39^2 2:05^1	Dwyer 56k	3	4	$3^{3\frac12}$	$1^{1\frac12}$	$1^{2\frac12}$	$1^{1\frac34}$	Guerin E	126	w	*.05	81-17	NativeDancer126$^{1\frac34}$[D]Dictar114^{2}GuardnII114^4	Much the best	5
13Jun53- 6Bel	fst 1½	:50^1 1:15 2:04^1 2:28^3	Belmont 118k	5	4	$3^{2\frac12}$	2^{hd}	1^{hd}	1^{nk}	Guerin E	126	w	*.45	95-11	NativeDancr126^{nk}JamieK.126^{10}RoylByGm126$^{4\frac12}$	Held gamely	6
	Geldings not eligible																
23May53- 7Pim	fst 1$\frac{3}{16}$	:47 1:11^4 1:38^2 1:57^4	Preakness 113k	4	3	3^3	2^{hd}	1^{hd}	1^{nk}	Guerin E	126	w	*.20	91-19	NativeDancer126^{nk}JamieK.126^{6}RoyalBayGem126^2	Hard drive	7
16May53- 6Bel	fst 1	:23^4 :47^1 1:11^3 1:36^1	Withers 32k	3	2	$2^{\frac12}$	$1^{\frac12}$	$1^{2\frac12}$	1^4	Guerin E	126	w	*.05	93-12	Native Dancer126^{4}Invigorator126$^{2\frac12}$Real Brother126	Easily	3
	Geldings not eligible																
2May53- 7CD	fst 1¼	:47^4 1:12^1 1:36^3 2:02	Ky Derby 118k	6	8	$4^{2\frac12}$	$4^{2\frac12}$	$2^{1\frac12}$	2^{hd}	Guerin E	126	w	*.70e	97-09	DarkStar126^{hd}NativeDancer126^{5}Invgortor126^2	Roughed,wide	11
25Apr53- 6Jam	fst 1⅛	:50 1:13^3 1:37^1 1:50^3	Wood Memorial 123k	4	2	3^1	2^{hd}	$1^{\frac12}$	$1^{4\frac12}$	Guerin E	126	w	*.10e	93-12	NativeDancer126$^{4\frac12}$TahitianKing126^{hd}Invigortor126^3	Easily	7
	Geldings not eligible																
18Apr53- 6Jam	fst 1$\frac{1}{16}$	:24^2 :49 1:13^4 1:44^1	Gotham (Div 1) 35k	8	4	$6^{2\frac34}$	$4^{1\frac14}$	2^{hd}	1^2	Guerin E	120	w	*.15	91-10	NatveDancr120^{2}MagicLmp120^{3}Sckl'sSound120$^{1\frac14}$	Ridden out	9
22Oct52- 6Jam	fst 1$\frac{1}{16}$	:24^2 :48 1:12^3 1:44^1	©East View 56k	1	4	4^6	3^3	$1^{\frac12}$	$1^{1\frac12}$	Guerin E	122	w	*.20	91-15	Native Dancer122$^{1\frac12}$Laffango122^{9}Teds Jeep122$^{1\frac12}$	Ridden out	6
	Geldings not eligible																
27Sep52- 6Bel	fst 6½f-W	:21^4 :44^2 1:08^2 1:14^2	Futurity 107k	8	6		5^4	$2^{\frac12}$	$1^{2\frac14}$	Guerin E	122	w	*.35	100-05	NativeDancer122$^{2\frac14}$TahitianKing122^{4}DarkStr122^3	Ridden out	10
	Geldings not eligible																
22Sep52- 5Bel	fst 6f-WC	:22 :44^3 1:09^3	Sp Wt 5000	6	6		5^3	1^2	$1^{1\frac14}$	Guerin E	118	w	*.40	93-07	NativeDancer118$^{1\frac14}$TahitianKing118$^{2\frac14}$Reprimnd118^{hd}	In hand	8
30Aug52- 6Sar	fst 6½f	:23^3 :48 1:12^3 1:18^4	Hopeful 62k	4	1	$6^{2\frac34}$	$5^{2\frac12}$	2^{hd}	1^2	Guerin E	122	w	*.25	91-19	Native Dancer122^{2}Tiger Skin122^{2}Platan122^1	Handily	7
23Aug52- 4Sar	fst 6f	:22^4 :46^2 1:11^1	Grand Union Hotel 20k	1	2	3^1	$1^{\frac12}$	$1^{1\frac12}$	$1^{3\frac12}$	Guerin E	126	w	*.55	92-17	NativeDancer126$^{3\frac12}$Laffango122$^{2\frac12}$TahitianKing122$^{5\frac12}$	In hand	5
16Aug52- 4Sar	sly 6f	:23^1 :46^4 1:13^1	Sar Spl 17k	4	2	$4^{2\frac12}$	4^2	1^1	$1^{3\frac12}$	Guerin E	122	w	*.70	82-22	NativeDancr122$^{3\frac12}$DocWalkr122^{4}SouthPont122$^{3\frac12}$	Ridden out	8
4Aug52- 6Sar	fst 5½f	:23^1 :47 :59^3 1:06	Flash 10k	5	4	3^1	3^1	$1^{\frac12}$	$1^{2\frac14}$	Guerin E	122	w	*.80	87-20	Native Dancer122$^{2\frac14}$Tiger Skin114^{2}Bradley122^{no}	Easily	7
23Apr52- 6Jam	fst 5f	:22^3 :46^3 :59^2	©Youthful 14k	4	2	2^1	2^{hd}	1^3	1^6	Guerin E	117	w	*.90	93-19	NativeDancr117^{6}Tribe122$^{1\frac12}$[DH]Mr.Mdnght117^1	Much the best	12
19Apr52- 2Jam	fst 5f	:23 :47 :59^3	Md Sp Wt	9	7	4^2	4^2	$1^{\frac12}$	$1^{4\frac12}$	Guerin E	118	w	*1.40	92-16	Native Dancer118$^{4\frac12}$Putney118^{nk}Khan118^{hd}	Drew out easily	9

Index

References

Chapter 1

1. Hoehling, A. A. & Mary. (1956). *The Last Voyage of the Lusitania*. New York: Henry Holt & Co., p.38.
2. Alfred Gwynne Vanderbilt papers. Courtesy National Museum of Racing, Saratoga Springs, N.Y.

Chapter 2

1. Paulick, Ray. "A racing man of the people," *The Blood-Horse*, November 20, 1999, p. 6945, and Hollingsworth, Kent, ed. (1970). *The Great Ones*. Lexington, Ky: The Blood-Horse, Inc., p. 91.
2. Paulick, Ibid.

Chapter 3

1. Palmer, Joe H. (Red Smith, ed.). (1953). *This Was Racing*. New York: A.S. Barnes & Co., p. 32.
2. Clippinger, Don, "Polynesian's Place in History, *The Thoroughbred Record*, May 15, 1985, pp. 2434-2435; Katz, Cathie, "Born to Run," *The Backstretch*, July/August 1998, pp. 96-98, 100; and Palmer, pp. 32-34.
3. Clippinger, p. 2435; and Palmer, p. 33.
4. Clippinger, Ibid.
5. Hirsch, Joe. (1996). *The First Century: Daily Racing Form Chronicles 100 Years of Thoroughbred Racing*. New York: Daily Racing Form Press, pp. 116-117.

Chapter 4

1. Shipman, Evan. (Charles Hatton, ed.). (1955). *The American Racing Manual*. Triangle Publications, p. 21. Copyrighted c. 2000 by Daily Racing Form, LLC. Reprinted with Permission of the Copyright owner.
2. Horwood, Bob. *The Morning Telegraph*. November 24, 1952. p. 4. Copyrighted c. 2000 by Daily Racing Form, LLC. Reprinted with Permission of the Copyright owner.
3. Hatton, Charles. (1953). *The American Racing Manual*. 1953 Edition. Triangle Publications, pp. 50-51. Copyrighted c. 2000 by Daily Racing Form, LLC. Reprinted with Permission of the Copyright owner.
4. Ibid. p. 51.
5. Ibid. p. 44.
6. Ibid. p. 52.

Chapter 5

1. McNulty, John. (David F. Woods, ed.). (1963). "A Room at the Barn." *The Fireside Book of Horse Racing: A Thoroughbred Treasury*. New York: Simon and Schuster, p. 217.
2. Hatton, Charles. (1954). *The American Racing Manual*. Triangle Publications, p. 54. Copyrighted c. 2000 by Daily Racing Form, LLC. Reprinted with permission of the Copyright Owner.
3. McNulty, pp. 218, 220.

4. *Louisville Times.* April 18, 1953.

5. Gay, Marvin N. Jr. *Louisville Times.* April 13, 1953.

6. Copyrighted c. 1999 by Daily Racing Form, LLC and Equibase Company. Reprinted with permission of the Copyright Owner.

Chapter 6

1. Smith, Red. *Louisville Times.* April 29, 1953.

2. Ruby, Earl. "Ruby's Report." *Louisville Courier-Journal.* April 28, 1953.

3. Smith. *Louisville Times.* May 2, 1953.

4. Ibid.

Chapter 7

1. I found nothing of Native Dancer tying-up in any of the contemporary sources I examined, but in an interview with Deirdre Biles, *The Blood-Horse*, April 17, 1993, p. 1883, Dr. Alex Harthill said that Native Dancer tied-up badly the day before the Derby.

2. Smith, Red. "Native Dancer's Influence Still Dominant." *Louisville Courier-Journal.* May 2, 1978; and "Native Dancer and the Derby." *The New York Times.* May 1, 1978.

3. Woods, ed. *The Fireside Book of Horse Racing.* p. 277.

Chapter 8

1. Gay, Marvin N. Jr. *Louisville Times.* May 6, 1953.

2. Putnam, Pat. "When Guerin and The Dancer Were out of Step." *Sports Illustrated*, October 15, 1973, p. S8.

3. Copyrighted c. 1999 by Daily Racing Form, LLC and Equibase Company. Reprinted with Permission of the Copyright owner.

4. Putnam. "When Guerin and The Dancer Were out of Step."

Chapter 9

1. Horwood, Bob. "Picking up the Pieces." *The Thoroughbred Record.* May 16, 1953. p. 9.

2. Ibid.

3. Copyrighted c. 1999 by Daily Racing Form, LLC, and Equibase Company. Reprinted with Permission of the Copyright owner.

4. Tracy, Len. "Recrowned at Pimlico." *The Thoroughbred Record.* May 30, 1953. p. 17.

5. Ibid.

Chapter 10

1. Robertson, William P. (1964). *The History of Thoroughbred Racing in America.* New York: Bonanza Books, p. 9.

2. Not to be confused with the Widener Course over which Native Dancer won the Futurity, and which replaced the original course installed in 1925 by track president Joseph E. Widener.

3. Shipman, Evan. (1955). *The American Racing Manual.* p. 22.

4. Dunn, Neville. "Commentary." *The Thoroughbred Record.* June 20, 1953.

Chapter 11

1. Putnam. "When Guerin and the Dancer Were out of Step."
2. Associated Press report, August 20, 1953.
3. Associated Press report, August 22, 1953.

Chapter 12

1. Shipman. (1955). *The American Racing Manual.* p. 23.
2. Strine, Gerry. "Room at the Top." *The Blood-Horse.* June 29, 1985. p. 4311.
3. *TIME.* May 31, 1954.
4. Hirsch, Joe. *The First Century.* p. 120.
5. Hollingsworth, Kent. "Native Dancer." *The Blood-Horse.* May 19, 1984. p. 3569.

Chapter 13

1. Hatton, Charles. (1955). *The American Racing Manual.* p. 53.
2. Arnold, Jobie. "In the Winner's Circle." *The Thoroughbred Record.* August 10, 1963.
3. Arnold. May 14, 1966. p. 1269.
4. Paraphrased from: Jim Bolus. (1993). *Kentucky Derby Stories.* Gretna, La: Pelican Publishing Co., p. 137.
5. Bolus. *Kentucky Derby Stories.* p. 139.

Epilogue

1. Warfield, Missy. "Joe Hall lives in Two Worlds." *The Maryland Horse.* p. 33.
2. Ibid.
3. Carter, Snowden. *The Maryland Horse.* December, 1967. p. 25; and Warfield, p. 33.
4. Joe Hall narrative from Carter. *The Maryland Horse.* December 1967. pp. 25-29.
5. Putnam. "When Guerin and The Dancer Were Out of Step." p. S6.
6. Robinson, Patrick. (1975). *Classic Lines.* Gretna, La: Oxmoor House, p. 149.
7. Hatton, Charles. *Daily Racing Form.* November 17, 1967. Copyrighted c. 2000 by Daily Racing Form, LLC. Reprinted with permission of the Copyright Owner.

Photo Credits

Cover photo: (Bert Morgan)

Page 1: Native Dancer's stride (*LIFE* Magazine); Dancer head shot (Bert Morgan)

Page 2: Unbreakable (Meadors Photo); Polynesian (Bert Morgan); Discovery (The Blood-Horse); Geisha (Meadors Photo)

Page 3: Old Sagamore (Courtesy of Mr. & Mrs. Ralph Kercheval); Sagamore in 1998 (Barbara D. Livingston)

Page 4: Alfred Vanderbilt and Bill Winfrey (Meadors Photo); Winfrey and Sunny Jim Fitzsimmons (Paul Schafer)

Page 5: Dancer in a van (Belmont Park); Dancer with Guerin up (Saratoga); Dancer with Arcaro up (Courtesy of Carey Winfrey); Jockey group photo (Courtesy of Al Popara)

Page 6-7: Dancer winning the Youthful, Flash, Saratoga Special, and Grand Union Hotel Stakes (all Bert Morgan)

Page 8: Dancer winning the Hopeful and Anticipation Purse (both Bert Morgan); Winning the East View (Empire City Photo)

Page 9: Dancer winning the Wood Memorial (The Blood-Horse); Kentucky Derby finish (Churchill Downs); Winning the Withers (Belmont Park)

Page 10: Dancer winning the Preakness; Preakness come back shot; Preakness winner's circle (all The Blood-Horse)

Page 11: Dancer winning the Belmont; Dancer and Vanderbilt post-Belmont; Winning the Dwyer (all Bert Morgan)

Page 12: Dancer winning the Arlington Classic and the Travers (both The Blood-Horse)

Page 13: Dancer winning the Metropolitan (Belmont Park); Being bathed at Saratoga (Brewer Photo); With Les Murray (Courtesy of Carey Winfrey)

Page 14: Natalma (The Blood-Horse); Sea-Bird (W.W. Rouch & Co.); Raise a Native (The Blood-Horse)

Page 15: Real Quiet (Barbara D. Livingston); Alysheba (E. Martin Jessee); Fusaichi Pegasus (Barbara D. Livingston); Thunder Gulch (Barbara D. Livingston)

Page 16: Native Dancer conformation (Winants Bros.); Gravestone (Courtesy of Mr. & Mrs. Ralph Kercheval)

Acknowledgments

My first and most heartfelt gratitude to my Heavenly Father, through His Son and my Lord, for the many good blessings and opportunities He has given me.

In more ways than one, this is a book long overdue, and right out of the gate I want to express my gratitude to editors Jacqueline Duke and Judy Marchman of Eclipse Press for giving me this opportunity and patiently enduring crashed computers, broken ribs, and torn ligaments. Overdue, because it is a story I have long wanted to tell.

My thanks to those who have helped along the way, and who are listed in the order I first pestered them: Alfred Gwynne Vanderbilt; Daniel W. Scott, on whose Lexington farm a legend was born; trainer William C. Winfrey and his son Carey, who helped me to know his late father better; Al Popara, who has borne the burden of "bad guy" for far too many years; and especially two very beautiful people, Mr. and Mrs. Ralph Kercheval, who shared wonderful moments in Native Dancer's life and theirs; and to their son, Ron Kercheval, and his photographer friend, Ta-o Irtz.

A world of thanks to Joe Hirsch, who shared his

priceless storehouse of memories; Field Horne at the National Museum of Racing and Tom Gilcoyne, for a look at 1950s Saratoga.

Thanks to those who never hung up on me when I called needing information yesterday: Cathy Schenck and Phyllis Rogers at the Keeneland Library; Diane Viert at *The Blood-Horse*; and Dorothy Ours at the National Museum of Racing. And to Lucy Acton of *The Mid-Atlantic Thoroughbred*; and Jennifer Lusk and Paula Welch of *Daily Racing Form*.

And to anyone my overloaded RAM has erased, my thanks and sincerest apologies.

AUTHOR

E va Jolene Boyd is a sixth-generation Texan. Born in San Antonio in 1937, she has loved horses her entire life. Assault was the first great racehorse she ever saw in person when she went to King Ranch. Boyd's own horses include a half-Thoroughbred and a little Mexican cow pony.

Boyd's love affair with Thoroughbred racing began in 1953 when saw the telecast of Native Dancer winning the Gotham Stakes. The Dancer hooked her for good and still remains her favorite.

She eventually combined her love for both horses and writing. She has had articles published in *The Thoroughbred Record, Turf and Sport Digest, SPUR, The Backstretch,* and *The Blood-Horse.*

Boyd also has had two previous books published: *That Old Overland Stagecoaching* and *Noble Brutes: Camels on the American Frontier.* She also is working on a book about cattle drives and ranching. She resides in Ingram, Texas.

175

Forthcoming titles
in the

THOROUGHBRED
Legends®

series:

Nashua

Spectacular Bid

John Henry

Personal Ensign

Available titles

Man o' War

Dr. Fager

Citation

Go for Wand

Seattle Slew

Forego

www.thoroughbredlegends.com

Editor — Jacqueline Duke
Assistant editors — Judy L. Marchman, Rena Baer
Book design — Brian Turner